"*Breaking Emotional Barriers to Heal*
Miller co-authored with Randy C
Healing Doesn't Happen. In this bool
nies of people who have been healed of chronic diseases. Craig has
found that the key to the physical healing is the release of suppressed emotions that occur as the result of trauma. Jesus makes
us whole—spirit, soul, and body. Jesus heals our soul and body.
Craig has a master's degree in social work. His experience in private practice and in his work at hospitals add levels of depth of
wisdom. The tools in this book expose and remove the emotional
roots of medical conditions. There are pearls of wisdom here for
all, but especially for those who pray for healing, and those who
have to contend to keep their healing."

—*David Zaritzky, MD*
Leader, Healing Ministry
Grace Church, High Point, NC

"Craig Miller's competence in the field of emotional healing is only
rivaled by his compassion. His new book is lending us permission
to ask questions that, until now, we would not have asked. The
book is a blueprint for the restoration of a sound mind, as well
as the healing of those physical and mental scars that hinder the
freedom that Christ came to give us. I am struck by the simplicity
by which Craig has written on such a complex topic. Craig's book,
while rooted in both scientific and empirical data, stands firm on a
practical theology that sees the whole person healed!"

—*Pastor Scott Caesar*
Founder/Men's Pastor, Men's Discipleship Network
mensdiscipleshipnetwork.com

"*Breaking Emotional Barriers to Healing* presents a practical, faith-filled approach allowing Christians to move with the power of the Holy Spirit to break free of emotional, physical, and spiritual affliction. Craig's nearly forty years of clinical and pastoral counseling experience provides a treasure trove of tools for everyday Christians to experience firsthand the perfect healing power of Jesus Christ. This is a must-read for every person seeking to see bondage and limitation removed from their lives, and in the lives of those around them."

—*Rev. Joanne Moody*
International speaker, author, healer
Agapefreedomfighters.org

"Craig Miller has created a powerful, practical tool to assist those who believe in the power of God to heal physical disease by exploring the root causes of much illness, pain, and seemingly 'incurable' physical distress. His research and experience as a therapist and speaker bring together this guide that everyone who prays for the sick will want to add to their toolbox of resources."

—*Dr. Mike Hutchings*
Director, Global School of Supernatural Ministry and the Global Certification Programs
Founder, God Heals PTSD Foundation
Author, *Soul Restoration: Healing the Wounds of Life and War*

"I consider myself a friend and fellow companion of Craig Miller on the journey God has led each of us to in healing ministry. In this book, Craig reveals the secret to healing and freedom: removing the obstacles and blockages in one's heart, being open here on earth, and being loved by the Bridegroom Jesus, His Father, and the Holy Spirit. I thank God for sending Craig into my life as a spiritual companion and teacher."

—*Fr. Jim Curtin*
Pastor, St. Dennis Catholic Church
Lockport, IL

BREAKING EMOTIONAL BARRIERS TO HEALING

UNDERSTANDING THE MIND-BODY CONNECTION TO YOUR ILLNESS

CRAIG A. MILLER

WHITAKER
HOUSE

This book is not intended to provide medical advice or to take the place of medical advice and treatment from your personal physician. Readers are advised to consult their own doctors or other qualified health professionals regarding the treatment of their medical problems. Neither the publisher nor the author takes any responsibility for any possible consequences from any treatment, action, or application of medicine, supplement, herb, or preparation to any person reading or following the information in this book. If readers are taking prescription medications, they should consult with their physicians and not take themselves off medicines to start supplementation without the proper supervision of a physician.

BREAKING EMOTIONAL BARRIERS TO HEALING:
Understanding the Mind-Body Connection to Your Illness

Insightsfromtheheart.com
talkwithcraig@juno.com

ISBN: 978-1-64123-117-6
eBook ISBN: 978-1-64123-118-3
Printed in the United States of America
© 2018 by Craig A. Miller

Whitaker House
1030 Hunt Valley Circle
New Kensington, PA 15068
www.whitakerhouse.com

Library of Congress Cataloging-in-Publication Data (Pending)

1 2 3 4 5 6 7 8 9 10 11 🄪 25 24 23 22 21 20 19 18

CONTENTS

FOREWORD

Have you ever prayed for someone's healing but afterward, either nothing happened or there was only a slight improvement? After you've worked up the courage to initiate prayer for someone's healing, it's easy to lose your nerve when nothing happens as a result, especially if you do not know what to do when healing does not happen. This is such an important topic that Craig and I co-authored the book *Finding Victory When Healing Doesn't Happen*, which addressed some important issues concerning when healing doesn't occur after prayer. We have continued to see an increase in interest from people hungry to receive more information about healing breakthrough.

I am so excited about three books that deal with both physical and emotional healing, books that, I feel, are going to be valuable toods for people who work and minister with those who suffer. Those three books are: *Soul Pain Revealed: The Mystery of Mentall Illness*, by Dr. Julie Caton; *Soul Restoration: Healing the Wounds of Life and War*, a forthcoming book by Mike Hutchings; and this book, *Breaking Emotional Barriers to Healing*.

Craig's experience as a Christian mental health therapist, and his passion to see people set free when healing doesn't occur, has prompted him to continue writing more on this subject. *Breaking Emotional Barriers to Healing* provides more insight about how physical, emotional, and cellular memory trauma can block the healing process and interfere with the spirit, soul, and body connections. He includes prayers to identify and release emotional issues that directly interfere with healing and with the restoration of your mind and body. This is also a guidebook for various issues that may occur during prayer, such as what to do when a person is not ready to forgive, not letting go of anger, not trusting Jesus to heal, not able use God's authority and power when praying, and much more. At the end of the book, there is a list of specific medical conditions and the underlying emotional roots related to each one.

Inner healing is a way of going through the process of sanctification and becoming what God says we are: free and forgiven. Inner healing can happen in different ways, and I believe it is important that everyone learn how to pray for the sick, and to know what to do when little or nothing changes after you pray. Because people typically do not know what to do when healing does not happen, Craig's book provides more awareness about identifying and releasing root issues for more healing breakthrough.

—*Randy Clark, D. Min.*
Overseer, Apostolic Network of Global Awakening
Founder, Global Awakening

PART I
UNDERSTANDING MIND-BODY
CONNECTIONS TO YOUR ILLNESS

1

HOW TRAUMA IMPACTS YOUR MIND AND BODY

As my wife and I were ministering at a healing conference, a thirty-one-year-old woman named Julie asked us to pray with her. Most of her life, she had been living with the intestinal pain of irritable bowel syndrome, severe foot problems, confusion, dizziness, and extreme fatigue. Within the past fifteen years, she had complained of back problems due to scoliosis, neck pain, ribs slipping out of place, poor leg circulation, an off-axis pelvic bone, and body tension. Within the last two years, she also suffered from headaches, uteral pain, and adrenal fatigue. Years of medical treatment had resulted in little to no results from doctors who could not find answers. As a prayer minister herself, even though she had a strong faith and loved seeing others healed, she had been unable to receive her own total healing. Although she knew God loved her, she also knew it did not make sense for her to live this way, and for her prayers not to remain unanswered. Julie reported that, with so many physical restrictions and medical problems, her life had never been "normal." The amount of emotional pain, sadness, stress, and fear she carried inside made it difficult for her to be strong for her own family.

As I listened, my heart grieved to hear about her years of emotional and physical suffering. It never seems to make sense why people must continue in misery, especially when they pray to a loving and merciful heavenly Father, and yet, they do not receive healing. But I also know she had many layers of unresolved emotional trauma and unhealthy beliefs that were among the causes of her relentless symptoms. I asked her if she was ready to revisit the past emotional wounds in her heart and mind that unknowingly affected her. She said she had already done some inner healing and was not sure what else to do. I told her that her continued suffering with pain and physical conditions was evidence that additional layers of emotional trauma needed to be revealed and released. She was open to allowing us to pray for her condition.

When we prayed together, God revealed hurt from various family members, and the emotional connection she still had to those situations. God started with an image of her mother's womb, and times of rejection from her parents, and the subsequent feelings of disapproval, unworthiness, fear, confusion, shame, and abandonment that were the result of years of abuse and neglect. Each time God reveal a trauma, Julie was able to release the emotions associated with that trauma. As a result, the pain from a body area associated with each expressed emotion began to decrease, until all her pain was gone. (The association between the body and emotions will be explained in more detail later.) When we asked God to restore the love, life, peace, significance, and identity she had not received from her parents, areas of her body literally began shifting and improving before our eyes. By the time we were done praying, Julie was able to walk away completely symptom-free! She was able to sleep through the night, felt no pain or fear, experienced clarity of thought, felt energetic, had normal bodily functions, believed in herself, and began to enjoy life in ways that she had been unable to do for most of her life.

I have heard so many stories like Julie's. Stories in which people had been hurting from a condition, emotionally and physically, for some time. After many unsuccessful attempts at healing, it is easy to become discouraged as you question what is wrong with you or your faith. Over time, you begin the downward spiral of wondering whether God wants you healed, or if you are destined to live this way forever. These thoughts and feelings are common because you cannot make sense of your lack of healing, especially when you hear messages of how much God loves you and wants you to be healed. In time, you come to believe that the only option available is to develop a new way of living with your painful condition, or you will begin shutting down in order to merely survive in a life of misery. This allows discouragement to fester, which causes additional unwanted symptoms, and distorts the truth that God *does* want you to be healed.

I believe God can heal anybody, anytime, anywhere, and that He created your body and mind to naturally work toward healing. So, the question I often hear is, "If God wants me well, why do I struggle to receive healing, or lose it as soon as I get it?"

I read that the well-known healing evangelist Kathryn Kuhman commented that only 10 to 15 percent of people keep their healing. That is an unfortunately low number of people who are able to experience permanent healing. This has significantly discouraged people from relying on prayer as a method of healing. However, it is my prayer and passion to see those numbers reversed, so that 90 percent of people are able to keep their healing. And from what God demonstrated to me through the healing prayers found in this book, I believe it is realistic to expect that 90 percent (or more) of those healed will keep their healing. One of the main purposes of this book is to help lay the groundwork for a practical understanding of what God wants you to know in order to break any and all barriers that keep permanent healing from taking place.

Sometimes, when people pray for healing and don't receive it, they think their prayers are not answered, and more importantly, they do not know what to do next in order to receive healing. This is a common issue, even in the church, especially since there is little spiritual teaching about the barriers that block your spirit, soul, and body from receiving healing. In the book I cowrote with Dr. Randy Clark, *Finding Victory When Healing Doesn't Happen*, we described some of the core reasons that can hinder the divine healing process, such as unworthiness, unbelief, fear, doubt, unforgiveness, sin, worldly expectations, curses, and spiritual warfare. (See chapter 11 for more details.) One of the most common hindrances to healing is past, unresolved emotional trauma that is held inside. In fact, emotional trauma is so powerful, if it is held inside long enough, it can weaken the body, make it more susceptible to illness, weaken your faith in healing, and block any healing of your specific symptoms!

Emotions are often overlooked when it comes to disease, pain, and the healing process.

In the many years I have prayed for and witnessed healings, especially for illnesses with long-term conditions, I have found that emotions are one of the most common, most misunderstood, and undertaught reasons for the lack of healing of mind-body illnesses. No matter what injury or condition you have, inner emotion is always part of the problem, but it is rarely discussed as part of the solution. This is among the reasons why the Centers for Disease Control and Provention (CDC) states that 85 percent of physical illness has an emotional root. That is an extremely high percentage for emotions to affect your state of health!

Your body has a great capacity to resist illness, especially when you care for yourself and do things like routinely releasing emotions, in order to balance your mind and regulate the body stress level. Even Scripture lets you know that when you confess, or let go of, your thoughts to one another, you may be healed. (See James 5:16.) However, when you hold in your intense emotions that result from accumulated hurt or trauma, your mind and body become stressed and out of balance. For example, among the bodily systems that are most affected by stress are the immune system, heart, and digestive system.[1] When these areas of your

1. Karol K. Truman, *Feelings Buried Alive Never Die…* (St. George, Utah: Olympus Distributing, 1991), 220–264.

body are functioning in a weakened state, you are more suseptible to illness and disease. This means your weakened systems will struggle to fight off illness, contribute to the cause of your illness, and even block your healing, especially with suppressed emotions. (See chapter 15 for more details).

Research details the influence of stress and the importance of expressing emotions to assist in healing and healthy living.

+ Up to 98 percent of mental, physical, and behavioral illness comes from our thought life[2]

+ Stress is a factor in 75 percent of all illnesses and diseases[3]

+ 88 of cancers are due to lifestyle and not genetics[4]

+ 75 to 90 percent of all visits to the primary care doctor are due to stress-related problems[5]

EARLIER TRAUMA CAUSES A GREATER INTENSITY OF PAIN

Hurtful physical and emotional events can happen any time in life. However, the earlier and the more severe the event, the more devastating the experience can be. When hurtful events happen, it forges a chainlink to you, like a steel ring welded to your soul. With each additional hurtful event, another steel ring is welded to your soul. As a result, you end up with a long chain of hurt and disappointment.

For about forty years, Martha experienced constant anxiety and complained of poor time management. She felt pressure each

2. Dr. Caroline Leaf, *Switch on Your Brain* (Grand Rapids, MI: Baker Books, 2013), 33.

3. Sheldon Cohen PhD, Denise Janicki-Deverts PhD, Gregory E. Miller PhD, "Psychological Stress and Disease," *JAMA*, October 10, 2007, 1685, https://jamanetwork.com/journals/jama/article-abstract/209083?redirect=true (accessed April 30, 2018).

4. International Agency for Research on Cancer and the World Health Organization, "Cancer Statistics and Views of Causes," *Science News*, vol. 115, no. 2 (January 13, 1979), 23.

5. Dr. Paul Rosch, "Stress and Heart Disease," http://www.stress.org/stress-and-heart-disease/ (accessed April 30, 2018).

morning to get activities done. If she did not hurry, she felt pressure in her head and anxiety in her stomach. God took her back to when she was ten years old and her mother would frequently yell at her, expressing disappointment, impatience, and, to Martha, a lack of love. As a result, Martha felt inadequate, unloved, anxious, and viewed herself as a constant source of disappointment to her parents. When she gave these feelings to God and forgave her family members, the anxiety and pressure disappeared. The emotion of those early years was so strong, it forged a chain link that lasted forty years, until she was finally ready to reveal it and release it.

If you do not work through your feelings, each hurt and disappointment from the important people in your life (a parent, friend, teacher, boyfriend or girlfriend, spouse, employer, etc.), will continue to create more rings on the chain of unhealthy emotions. With each hurt, the chain becomes heavier and the feelings more intense. This accumulation of hurt from physical and/or emotional trauma will greatly affect how you feel inside emotionally, what you will believe about your healing, and how you will react to other people or situations. For example, the longer you hold in emotions from unresolved (unhealed) past hurts and carry around unforgiveness, the greater chance you will struggle with believing in your healing and experience issues such as:

+ an increase in emotional and physical illnesses

+ chronic conditions and unsuccessful healing

+ feelings of being unworthy, unforgivable, or undeserving of healing

+ doubt that God can use you to heal others

+ a belief that your prayers are ineffective

+ a belief that you must live with your symptoms and healing is not for you

+ a belief that God wants you to suffer in order to learn something

If you are experiencing any of these common issues, you are not alone. So many people are being deceived because of unresolved negative emotions that create ungodly beliefs, fears, and lies from past hurts. These unhealthy perceptions, created through hurtful experiences, become your reality and corrupt your ability to believe the truth about receiving healing, as well as your authority to minister healing to others. The good news is that you don't have to live with these issues. You can learn new ways to reveal and release what is not of God and receive what God wants you to have.

A woman named Mary was not healed after we prayed for her a few times. When I asked if she wanted to be healed, Mary said she felt there was a difference between wanting to be healed and expecting to be healed. Mary said she didn't know how God would want to heal someone like her, since she didn't feel she was "good enough" to be healed. When I asked how she felt when she said that, Mary said she felt sadness and rejection.

God took Mary to a childhood memory of lying in bed when she was sick. Since her mother was always busy, Mary's childhood was filled with sad, lonely, bored, and rejected feelings because of her mother's neglect. This experience created Mary's belief that she was not good enough to be cared for, and her mother's lack of love created Mary's feeling of being unworthy of good things. When Mary released her hurt, sad, and empty feelings, she realized her adult feelings of being lonely, sad, and not good enough were the same ones she had as a child. As she envisioned Jesus giving her His love through a hug, Mary saw herself sitting up in bed and feeling better. Next, she envisioned Jesus laughing and having fun, even jumping on the bed with her. I could see Mary's face light up as she realized the truth about herself.

THE IMPORTANCE OF EMOTIONS

The importance of emotions cannot be ignored, since research has shown they are necessary to assign value, purpose, and meaning to what you do. Emotions bring the whole body into a single purpose, integrating systems and coordinating mental processes and biology to create behavior.[6]

Even the Bible references the emotional life of Jesus Christ during His time of ministry. Scripture states we are to be imitators of God. (See Ephesians 5:1.) Since Jesus was the best Imitator of what God wants us to be like, God wants you to also show the emotions of Jesus, such as grief (see Matthew 26:38), fear and agony (see Luke 22:44), anger (see John 2:15), tears (see John 11:35), rejection (see John 19:15), and joy (see Luke 10:21). My point is, if you want to be like Jesus, and if you want to maintain a healthy life, you must similarly identify and express emotions as Jesus did.

Since the apostle Paul was also one of the best imitators of Jesus, he wrote, *"Whatever you have learned or received or heard from me, or seen in me—put it into practice. And the God of peace will be with you"* (Philippians 4:9 NIV). So when you express your feelings, which is how God designed you to function, you will begin to find the peace, joy, and healing that God intended for you to experience.

Your God-given emotions are vitally important to how you live. Although you cannot control the events or circumstances that bring fear, lies, and illness, you can choose to control what you will do with your emotions to influence your healing. The Scriptures let you know: You do not have a spirit of fear but of love, power, and a sound mind. (See 2 Timothy 1:7 KJV.) You have a choice. Either you can take control of illness or your illness will take control of you. In the subsequent chapters, you will learn more about how to take control of your emotions and illnesses in order to obtain successful and permanent healing.

---

6. Leaf, 88.

2

WHAT HAPPENS WHEN THERE IS EMOTIONAL TRAUMA

Roger was in severe pain as he sat in front of me asking for prayer. Part of him was hoping for healing, but another part of him was filled with doubt. His desperation to try anything came from the suffering he had endured for the past thirty-five years, after his motorcycle was hit by a drunk driver. As he described the accident, the look on his face revealed the sadness and strain that had accompanied a pain-filled life. He said the accident "blew out" his spine, knocked out a disc, partially severed his leg, broke many ribs, and punctured his lung. Over the years, Roger had showed some improvement, but he believed many of his prayers had gone unanswered because he still endured a level of pain that severly impacted his quality of life. He still had to deal with severe back pain and impaired mobility due to the fact that one leg an inch shorter than the other. When I asked him to describe his pain level on a scale of zero to ten (ten being most painful), he said it was always a fifteen! Over the years, he had stopped taking prescribed pain medication because of the toll they had on his body and mind.

Roger did not know what else to do and was at the end of his rope. The doctors claimed there was nothing else they could do for him, besides prescribing more pain medication. He feared facing the disappointment of asking for prayer if healing didn't happen.

He was at the point where he questioned his faith and wondered whether God wanted him to be healed.

I told Roger that these were normal responses from an abnormal amount of trauma and suffering. I told him God was also saddened he was living this way, and God wanted Roger healed even more than Roger did. For people like Roger, who have endured a succession of disappointments, I first ask if they still want to be healed. If the person says no, or is hesitant to answer, I ask why they feel that way. I examine their answer to see if they reveal other issues that may be blocking their healing. Since Roger said yes to this question, I told him we would work together to discover what was blocking his healing.

I asked Roger to recall his accident and to picture Jesus standing between him and the accident site. I then commanded the emotional, physical, memory, and sight trauma to leave Roger, in Jesus's name. As Roger released the trauma and forgave the other driver, I asked God to adjust Roger's legs. As we both watched his shorter leg lengthen, he could feel his hips automatically adjust—and his back pain completely disappeared. Instantly, Roger was able to stand, walk, bend, and touch his toes without pain!

EVERY HURT OR WOUND IS A TRAUMA TO YOUR SYSTEM

Regardless of how you are able to relate with Roger's experiences, I do know that life is still full of hurt and pain that can greatly affect your body (physical) and soul (mind, will, and emotions). You must realize that any wound or hurt you receive (emotional or physical) is some form of trauma to your system.

The word *wound* is the English translation of the Greek word *trauma*, which is why I use the word *trauma* throughout the book and when I pray for healing. You can still use words such as *hurt*, *wounded*, *injured*, *abused*, *mistreated*, or others, but they are all trauma. Trauma comes in many forms.

Physical trauma can be from direct harm or injury to your body, including physical abuse, accidents, injuries, and even surgeries.

Corresponding with physical trauma is *cellular memory trauma*. When there is physical trauma to the body, your tissues, cells, muscles, ligaments, and organs all hold the memory of the trauma as living, sensing organisms.

Emotional trauma is the negative feelings associated with experiencing physical trauma. These feelings include such pain, fear, and sadness. Emotional trauma can also stem from hurtful verbal expressions toward you. (For more information, see the section on Misunderstood Domestic Violence Trauma in chapter 11.)

Other traumas may include: *sight trauma* from seeing devastation or something upsetting, such as seeing your father become angry when you are a child; *hearing trauma* from sounds that are frightening; or *general memory trauma*, which may include one traumatic event or an accumulation many traumatic memories over time. Whether you label the hurtful experiences wounds or trauma, it is all the same pain and suffering that needs to be revealed and released for your mind and body restoration. You will learn more details about these traumas throughout the book.

EVERY HARMFUL EVENT CREATES PHYSICAL TRAUMA

If you experience phsycially harm, your body will sustain physical trauma and cellular memory trauma with any type of bodily physical injury. Since everything in your body is living, every cell of your muscles, ligaments, organs, skin, etc., will carry the pain of an injury (cellular memory trauma) until you release the trauma. This can also include bodily injuries you do not remember. For example, forceful birthing experiences and prolonged time in the birth canal can create fears and anxieties. Even when you go under anesthesia during an operation, your body can experience cellular memory trauma. There are many testimonies of people who have had years of bodily pain after a surgerical procedure that was intended to relieve pain. As a result, however, the pain continued or was made worse. When the person pictured the surgerical event and commanded the cellular memory to leave, the pain disappeared.

There was a man who had surgery to repair a tear in his ACL knee ligament. After the surgery, he began to feel constant pain, which he reported as a six pain level. I had the man visualize himself on the operating table during the operation. I asked him to picture Jesus putting His hand over the knee, and as I commanded the physical and cellular memory trauma to leave, his pain disappeared. When I asked what happened after the surgery, he said he felt pain at a number eight and he had a lot of fear. Since fear is an open door for pain, I had him picture Jesus standing next to him in the recovery room. Then we commanded the fear to leave and asked Jesus to be a shield of comfort, life, and light. The pain and fear were gone.

EVERY HARMFUL EVENT CREATES EMOTIONAL TRAUMA

Whenever you are physically or emotionally hurt, there is always an emotional reaction (or *emotional trauma*). You can feel shock, hurt, saddness, fear, anger, and agitatation as a result of the event. The more hurtful sensations during or after the event, the greater the trauma imprint that is burned into your memory, and the more fears you will have of being harmed in future incidents.

For example, your father's angry face and the pain you felt as his belt hit your body while being disciplined would create many trauma sensations. During the Steps for Healing Prayer (see chapter 10 for details), I command all memories of emotion, sight, and sounds, as well as other physical and cellular memory trauma, to leave in Jesus's name. I declare healing and wholeness over each of those areas.

Bill sustained a hairline fracture when his car rolled over during an auto accident. Four years later, his wrist was constantly at a number four pain level. The pain ran up his arm to his shoulder, limiting movement of his arm and wrist. By the end of each day, his wrist reached a number ten pain level. For various reasons, Bill did not receive treatment at the time of the accident, and doctors now said nothing could be done. Bill would have to live with the pain, which would eventually progress into arthritis.

Over the years, Bill had received prayer with little result. I asked him to picture the accident in his mind, with Jesus protecting him. Next, I asked him to release all 'feeling words' about the incident to Jesus. As he did so, he released the fear and hurt he had experienced before, during, and after the accident. We prayed that his diagnosis would be removed. He forgave the other driver, and we commanded his wrist to be healed. Immediately, his pain reduced to a level two. Since Bill still experienced pain, I knew that additional emotion had to be released. When Bill released his disappointment due to living with the condition for the past four years, I commanded any leftover pain to leave in the name of Jesus. Bill walked away pain free. Praise God!

EVERY HARMFUL EVENT CREATES A BELIEF AND IMPACTS YOUR FAITH

Your belief system begins at an early age. The imprinting of memory and emotion occurs at this most vulnerable time of life. As a result, a hurtful event can create two major beliefs. First, you feel a lack of safety and a vulnerability to other people and to your environment. This is especially evident with people who are too distrustful for you to express emotions, afraid to be vulnerable with their emotions before others and God. Second, you develop negative beliefs about yourself, such as...

+ *I am bad.*

+ *I'm not good enough.*

+ *I'm afraid of conflict.*

+ *I don't deserve good things.*

+ *I fear authority figures.*
+ *I'm expected to suffer.*

Living with unhealthy thoughts and negative emotions distorts your perceptions of the truth and creates a crisis in your level of faith. Belief is what you use to define youself; faith is the action you display to express it. If you harbor negative beliefs about yourself or your feelings, you will not have the confidence to feel anything or do anything, and you will not be able to move forward.

Annie came to see me after years of feeling depressed and a lifetime of being afraid to accomplish things because she believed she would not be good enough. When I used the Steps for Healing Prayer, God took Annie back to an image of her fourth-grade teacher telling the class to be creative and make anything they wanted out of clay. Little Annie was so proud to show her teacher the bowl and lid she made. Her teacher said, "This is too small and would not hold up." With that, Annie saw the teacher crush the clay lid into the bowl. Annie described the event as devastating, leaving her feeling crushed, not good enough, and without the confidence that she could accomplish things. She realized that her childhood experience was the starting point for her negative beliefs that discouraged her from stepping out in faith. When she asked Jesus to stand between her and the teacher for protection, she was able to release the emotion, release the negative beliefs, and forgive the teacher. Annie felt an immediate release from her depression.

Many times, it only takes the words from one influential person early in life to make the most significant difference for good or for harm. Scripture states there is death and life in the power of the tongue. (See Proverbs 18:21.)

HOW THIS RELATES TO HEALING

These unhealthy perceptions or beliefs created through harmful experiences become reality, and they corrupt your ability to believe the truth about receiving healing, as well as your authority to heal others.

Scripture tells us that what you think affects who you are. (See Proverbs 23:7.) Perceptions created early in life can become your normal pattern of living, which can intensify unhealty beliefs, as well as feelings of guilt, doubt, unworthiness, fear, lovelessness, anxiety, abandonment, vulnerablity, and much more. This makes it harder to receive what God has for you, because...

+ You feel it is unsafe to let your guard down and let people or God into your heart.

+ You doubt healing can happen.

+ You feel unworthy to receive healing or God's love.

+ You feel unlovable or unwanted by God.

+ You feel afraid to risk being hurt again.

The list of lies goes on and on.

The most common of these ungodly belief imprints are feelings of being inadequate, unlovable, and unsafe. These create another lie that makes you afraid to be honest with your feelings, and ultimately, unworthy to receive healing. Even for those who do receive healing, unhealthy beliefs can make you struggle to maintain your healing, or feel worthy to receive more of God's love and favor.

In addition, past unresolved pain caused by important people who die, or those who leave you, neglect you, or abuse you, can create many unhealthy fears, which can transfer into adulthood. These people feel unlovable, abandoned, betrayed, struggle to get emotionally close, and have trouble trusting others, including God. Unless you release these emotions, they can become the foundation for what you believe the rest of your life. For example, if you felt unsafe and afraid when a parent yelled at you, you will have the tendency to believe that anyone who raises their voice is unsafe. The following diagram shows the progression of trauma, and the negative results that trauma creates.

Physical Trauma	creates —>	Emotional Trauma	creates —>	False Beliefs	creates —>	Reactions to Life and Healing
Mother shouts insults; father leaves home	—>	Fear, rejection, abandonment	—>	People are unsafe. Unable to trust.	—>	Cannot trust peopl or God to help or hea Afraid to g emotionall close

To heal the heart, correct the beliefs, and change a person's reactions to life, it is important to create an environment for the person to feel safe enough to release the emotional trauma. This is done during the Steps for Healing Prayer, which will be explained in more detail in chapter 10.

Since the unhealthy emotional trauma events are part of creating unhealthy beliefs and unforgiveness, releasing the original hurt is important, and will often automatically release the ungodly beliefs that make forgiving easier. Difficulty in letting go of ungodly beliefs (i.e, unworthiness, lack of confidence, etc.) and the inability to forgive are evidence that additional unhealthy emotions need to be revealed and released. The subsequent chapters will give more details on how to recognize, reveal, and release unhealthy emotions.

3

SUPPRESSED EMOTIONS ARE LINKED TO MIND-BODY ILLNESS

When hurtful experiences are processed correctly, the emotional, physical, and mental information is integrated in the mind and stored, to be used for current or future reactions. When you experience excessive unhealthy emotions (trauma) at one time, the mind cannot properly process all the information. As a result, the emotion, images, sounds, and physical sensations become stuck in a traumatic state, and the mind suppresses the information in order to protect the mind and body from shock. In addition, if your early caregivers did not model how to release emotions, or if you were discouraged from releasing the emotions you felt, it is only natural that you will hold in (suppress) your unhealthy emotions. Over time, your suppressed emotions are stored throughout the body in cells, muscles, tendons, and body systems,[7] creating a weakened state of functionality that makes the body more susceptible to illness and less capable or receptive to healing.

Some of the telltale signs indicating that you may have suppressed emotions:

+ Your feelings are numb and/or you have no or very limited emotional response.

---

7. Peter Chappell, *Emotional Healing with Homoeopathy* (Rockport, MA: Element, 1994), 23.

- You cannot remember or have periodic lapses of childhood memories.

- It is very difficult to express emotions and/or you become silent with others.

- You become defensive and/or have an emotional outburst of anger.

- You become "tongue tied" in a conversation and have difficulty knowing what to say.

- You fear conflictual situations or are afraid to share your thoughts and feelings.

- You cannot verbalize internal emotion (i.e., anxiety, sadness).

- Emotional and physical symptoms do not improve with medical and spiritual methods.

- Your behaviors, thoughts, and emotions become insensitive, erratic, abusive, or irrational.

The longer unresolved, unhealthy emotions remain, the greater the potential for the body to develop other unhealthy issues, such as increasing stress levels, disconnection of the body/soul/spirit, changing DNA structures, and emotional and physical illness. If you do not make corrective changes, you will not only suffer with the aforementioned unhealthy issues the rest of your life, but you will also pass the unhealthiness to the next generation.

STRESS

Although a certain amount of stress is normal, and can help you to be more alert, excessive amounts of stress lead to bodily, emotional, and mental harm. Stress can increase the risk of stroke, heart attack, ulcers, impaired sleeping, job performance issues, and mental illnesses such as depression, anxiety, and even symptoms of PTSD.[8] The best way to decrease stress is through proper care of yourself, such as regular exercise, good diet, less work pressure,

8. https://en.wikipedia.org/wiki/Psychological_stress (accessed May 17, 2018).

and especially free expression of your thoughts and feelings with safe and positive people.

John said to me, "I'm stuck in my life." He felt stressed at his job, which made him question his desire to be there. John's lack of confidence made him frequently feel as though he "messed up" in his job. He felt helpless to change things. He admitted to having few goals in life and had a hard time trusting God to comfort him when he felt anxious about trying new things. As a result, John felt unhappy, unmotivated, and hopeless about the future.

Given John's mature age and capabilities, I knew from the words he used to express his feelings that he suffered from unresolved childhood traumas. God took John to a memory of when he was five years old and his older siblings left home. He remained alone, as the only child of parents who were unemotional and often physically absent. His homelife created imprints that included: fear of people leaving (abandonment), uncertainty about life (hopelessness), fear of darkness (being alone), the inablity to do anything about his circumstances (helplessness), and a lack of comfort from his parents (insignificance). After asking God to reveal past trauma, and releasing the corresponding unhealthy emotions, John felt different and was able to accept good things from God. When we prayed for God to give him healthy emotions and a new perspective, he realized that his uncertainty in life situations (such as in his job) could be replaced with certainty, just by asking Jesus to provide comfort and confidence.

It was necessary to release the unhealthy past emotion before John could receive (and accept) revelation from God that would bring comfort to his situation. Unhealthy emotional imprints in childhood will always become a stronger influence than your more logical adult thoughts and behaviors. As a result, if the people you pray for display immaturity in their actions, words, and beliefs, this is confirmation that they have childhood issues that need to be revealed and released before they will believe healing will happen.

The Steps for Healing Prayer will also help to identify and release these issues.

SUPPRESSED EMOTION DISCONNECTS YOUR BODY/SOUL/SPIRIT

Suppressed emotion disconnects you from the spirit, interrupting your ability to hear, feel, sense God, or to believe in your ability to be healed and your authority to heal others. When you experience a hurtful (traumatic) event, especially before the age of twelve (prior to puberty), the emotions from that trauma can become stuck at your level of emotional development when the event occurred. If the child does not receive help to release the unhealthy emotion, the emotion will become suppressed and held deep inside. As a result, the adult person is destined to react emotionally at the same immature level of emotional development, unless traumatic emotions are dealt with. This is the reason you see people react immaturely, and at a greater level of intensity than seems appropriate, given the current triggering incident.

When you are emotionally stuck at an immature level of reaction, you cannot think past the emotion you feel. For example, if a loved one died or left home when you were six years old, the emotional pain and fear from the sense of loss and abandonment you experienced at that age can become the same emotion that will not allow you to trust God for healing as an adult. The more childhood emotion is suppressed inside, the more you cannot hear from God or believe in your healing, because the consuming emotions take over your ability to hear or make sense beyond the emotion. As a result, you will believe, feel, and react out of the childhood emotion, rather than from your logical beliefs and reactions as an adult.

This is what can make praying for an immature or emotionally shut-down person more difficult. They cannot hear or believe the truth about their healing, and they may interpret what the praying person says (or what God wants them to know) as a critique and judgment rather than direction and guidance. This is because they are emotionally stuck at the age of an earlier incident, perhaps when an authority figure was judgmental and wounded them. This hinders their ability to grow beyond the emotional lies they feel or the beliefs they hold. For example, you are reacting emotionally immature when you:

+ doubt, criticize, degrade, question, judge; unable to believe in your abilities or your healing.

+ say or hear words such as *doubt, can't, unfair, afraid, hopeless, helpless, not good enough, bad, unwanted, unloved, stupid, lost,* or *empty.*

+ do not believe in your destiny, gifts, talents, and abilities.

+ do not freely receive/give words or actions of affection, such as, hugs, kisses, or saying, "I love you."

+ become defensive, sarcastic, judgmental, emotionally shut down, with temper tantrums such as anger outbursts, slamming doors, crying spells, silent treatment, yelling, and arguing.

When you hear or see the aforementioned reactions with the prayee, it is important to listen and watch their words and behaviors to pick up where they are wounded. You can also have the prayee identify the emotions during the incident and use the Steps for Healing Prayer.

A women was crying in my office as she expressed how she was not good enough to be loved by God. Since I knew this type of belief originated in childhood, I asked her about her relationship with her parents. She replied that her mother was not loving to her and became jealous if she (as a little girl) tried to get close to her father. When I asked her to picture herself as a little girl, with Jesus standing between her and her parents, she suddenly felt protected. She realized it was not her fault that she did not receive love from her parents. When I asked her what she saw Jesus doing with the little girl, she pictured Him putting His arm around her. I gave the woman a small pillow to hug as she pictured Jesus hugging her. As I put my hand on her head to pray a Father's blessing over her, she began to cry again, but this time with the joy of feeling loved and cherished by a Father.

DNA CHANGES

Your DNA contains the genetic information that allows all modern living things to function, grow, and reproduce. DNA is a molecule that carries the genetic instructions used in the growth, development, functioning, and reproduction of all known living organisms, including many viruses.[9] DNA is the infrastructure that operates the cell structures and connects to all the cells throughout your body. It serves as the main communication network throughout the body. Your emotions program your DNA and shape the immune system of your cells. Negative emotions destroy the coherence of the immune system, while positive emotions enhance it.[10] In her book, *Switch on Your Brain*, Dr. Caroline Leaf reports on a study by the HeartMath Institute, which stated that thoughts and feelings of anger, fear, and frustration caused DNA to change shape according those thoughts and feelings. The DNA responded by switching off many of their codes, which reduced quality expression, and, in turn, produced physical shutdown due to the negative emotions.[11] Dr. Leaf does bring some good news: the negative shutdown or poor quality of the DNA codes were reversed by increased feelings of love, joy, appreciation, and gratitude![12]

---

9. http://altered-states.net/index2.php?/cart/index.php?main_page=product_info&products_id=1556 (accessed May 17, 2018).

10. http://www.soulsofdistortion.nl/SODA_chapter9.html (accessed May 17, 2018).

11. Caroline M. Leaf, *Switch On Your Brain* (Grand Rapids, MI: Baker Books, 2013) 35.

12. Ibid.

As I've stated, the expression of emotion is one of the greatest influences to either impeding your health or maintaining a healthy physical well-being and a relationship with God. The good news is, you have the ability to take charge of your health as you learn to reveal and release the unhealthy emotions and restore what is healthy. The next two chapters will continue to explain more about how suppressed emotions can be at the root of physical and mental illness.

4

EMOTIONAL CONNECTIONS TO PHYSICAL ILLNESS

For thirty years, Joyce suffered from pain and stiffness in her neck, shoulders, knee, and lower back. She expressed her pain at a level of eight. Previous medical treatment and prayers were unsuccessful to relieve the pain that limited her activities and increased her fear of experiencing more pain. Several years ago, she began to experience anxiety at a level of five to eight. When I asked God to take her back to a time when she first felt this type of anxiety, God took her back to scary memories of her father yelling at her when she was four years old. When I asked her to picture Jesus standing between her and her dad as a protector, we prayed for the emotional trauma to leave, and for God's peace and comfort for that little girl. After she released the fear, another memory of a family member being physically abusive came to her mind. She again pictured Jesus protecting her and safely being able to release the physical pain and emotional fear. When we prayed for physical healing, the pain disappeared and she had full movement in her arms and legs without restrictions. As she was leaving, she bent over to pick up a tissue and stood up with a smile. She excitedly held up the tissue, saying, "Wow, I didn't realize what I just did. I just picked up this tissue. I haven't been able to do that for years!"

As with Joyce's case, when the emotion you experience is too overwhelming, your mind will automatically withhold (suppress) that emotion. In his book *The Mindbody Prescription*, Dr. John Sarno emphasizes that suppression of hurtful emotion is a natural reaction of the brain to assist the mind and body from becoming too overwhelmed by physical trauma. When emotions become overwhelming, the mind produces physical symptoms that keep your attention focused on your body, and not on the feelings that are so unbearable.[13] In addition, when there is a physical injury, if the emotional trauma is not released, the mind will suppress the emotion, which can block the physical trauma from releasing. The physical trauma will be intensified to keep the focus on the physical condition and avoid having to experience the hurtful emotions. The longer the emotions are suppressed, the more physical conditions will appear throughout the weaker body parts in order to divert attention away from the original emotional source. The following are two ways your mind and body react to suppressed emotion:

1. SYMPTOMS WITH A KNOWN CAUSE

One of the most common reasons for painful physical and emotional conditions is due to emotional trauma caused by physical injuries in the past. If your current treatment is primarily focused on your physical symptoms, little to no attention will be paid to the emotional (soul) part of the injury. As a result, if only your physical body is attended to, while your soul (mind, will, and emotions) is ignored, any attempts at healing by either traditional medicine or prayer can be less effective. Even though God is able to heal through your prayers, He also gave you emotions that can override your ability to trust in spiritual healing. Thus, if you are consumed with medical treatment for your physical conditions, and your damaged emotions are not addressed, your physical symptoms may not be relieved.

With every physical injury, there is cellular memory trauma imprinted in the body (typically, but not always, relating to the

---

13. John E. Sarno, MD, *The Mindbody Prescription* (New York, NY: Warner Books, 1998), 18.

injury location) and the emotional memory trauma imprinted in the mind and heart. These imprints will lock physical trauma within the body, blocking its physical release for healing. This is among the reasons why treatment and prayer for physical symptoms may not permanently eliminate those symptoms. This typically creates more doubt and weakens your faith to believe in healing. However, when the various memory traumas are released and healed, the physical symptoms are also free to release, and often, healing automatically occurs. Even in cases in which I have prayed for someone who has experienced physical symptoms or pain with unsuccessful medical or spiritual intervention for up to fifty years, when I used the Steps for Healing Prayer, the physical symptoms disappeared, often without additional prayer for the physical condition.

A woman was born with a deformed curvature of the spine and, for thirty years, she experienced varying degrees of back pain, depending on the amount of stress in her life. At the time of our prayer, she indicated that her lower back pain was at a level four. When I asked her about the major stressors in her life, she said she had an abusive husband and memories of an abusive ex-boyfriend. As she released the different emotional and memory traumas, her back pain decreased with each trauma released. When we finally prayed for God to adjust her vertebra, God straighten her back and the pain left.

2. SYMPTOMS WITH AN UNKNOWN CAUSE

Suppressed symptoms can be experienced through various forms of emotional or physical conditions that can be considered *psychosomatic illness*. These are described as "a physical disease that is thought to be caused, or made worse, by mental factors. The term is also used when mental factors cause physical symptoms but where there is no physical disease."[14] These disorders are

---

14. "Psychosomatic Disorders," The Center for Treatment of Anxiety and Mood Disorders, http://centerforanxietydisorders.com/treatment-programs/psychosomatic-disorders/ (accessed May 18, 2018).

created by the unconscious mind to distract the conscious mind when emotions are too devastating to handle.[15] The symptoms can be either temporary or, more typically, chronic conditions if the unhealthy emotions are never released. Traditional medical treatment focused on physical symptoms has little success with total healing, since these symptoms are typically emotional in origin. These types of emotional symptoms can also interfere with healing through prayer. (This will be discussed later.) Among the best treatments is to reveal and release the emotions from past stressful issues of life and/or identify the emotions that are experienced from living with the current condition. The following are only some stress-related illnesses that include physical and emotional conditions:

+ lower back, leg, neck, shoulder, arm, head (migraine) pain
+ disorders involving muscle, tendon, or body conditions with chronic pain
+ gastrointestinal, circulatory, skin, immune, cardiovascular, and neurological systems
+ anxiety, panic, and Obsessive Compulsive Disorder (OCD)
+ many depressive disorders, dissociative disorders, and bipolar symptoms
+ many issues related to sleep, diet, allergies, and addictions

There was a woman who had been experiencing pain in her knees for several months. She could not figure out why the condition started. Since there was no specific incident or origin, I asked her what it felt like to live with that condition. She said she felt restricted, stuck, helpless to do anything, and unable to move forward in life. Since I knew those words did not match her maturity level and lifestyle, the Holy Spirit was telling me there were more issues in her past. (Even if you do not get an impression from the Holy Spirit, you can still ask questions about their past.) As the

---

15. John E. Sarno MD, *The Divided Mind* (New York: HarperCollins, 2006), 12.

woman searched her memory, she saw the image of her as a child when her parents were strict and placed high expectations on her to care for her siblings while they worked. She realized that she was still experiencing the childhood feelings of being restricted, stuck, and helpless. When she pictured Jesus standing and protecting her, she was able to release these aforementioned feelings and forgive her parents. Her knee pain disappeared.

EMOTIONS LINKED TO BODY CONDITIONS

Science tells us that everything is constantly vibrating and emitting sound. Vibration is what makes it possible for things to exist, and everything that exits is in a state of vibration.[16] Even our Creator made the first vibration with the first sound when He said, "Let there be light" (Genesis 1:3), and there was light. Every part of the human body vibrates at a specific frequency, called *resonance*. According to Dr. Dennis Cousino, naturopathic physician, international speaker, and founder of Dynamic Health, if that vibration freaquency is out of balance, disease occurs as a result, and when your body is in a healthy balanced state, your body resonates at a healthy harmonic balance and vibration. However, suppressed unhealthy stress or emotions held in the body will produce an unhealthy vibrational frequency, which causes a state of disharmony that, in essence, is a state of disease and illness in the body. Emotions like sadness, anger, frustration and jealousy emit a lower freaquency, whereas the expression of love and joy emit the highest freaquency. The words you speak have the power to carry life or death into your existence. (See Proverbs 18:21.)

Since each organ and emotion has a vibrational frequency that resonate at similar frequencies, if the unhealthy emotion is not released, they will settle in the body organ or area with a similar frequency. As a result, disease can occur in that body organ when unhealthy emotional frequency forces the body's vibrational frequency to drop below a certain point. For example, resonating

16. Masaru Emoto, *The Miracle of Water* (New York: Atria Books, 2007), 30.

frequency of the emotion fear resonates at a similar frequency as the kidney. As a result, long-term suppression of fear is believed to influence illness conditions within the kidney. If the kidney is already at a weakened state from a medical ailment, the unhealthy frequency will make the illness worse, or it can prevent the kidney from recovering, even with conventional medical treatment. In such cases, healing prayer may be less effective, especially if the fear is overpowering the person's faith to believe. The following chart shows some of the emotion-organ links to illness. You will read a comprehensive list of emotion-organ links in chapter 15, "Suggested Emotional Connection to Mind-Body Conditions."

RELATIONSHIP OF EMOTION WITH BODY FUNCTION

AFFECTED ORGAN(S)	EMOTIONAL CONNECTION
Bladder	Fear
Gallbadder	Resentment
Heart	Imbalanced joy
Kidney	Fear
Liver	Anger
Lung	Grief
Pineal, Brain, Nerve System, Hypothalamus	Discouragement
Spleen / Pancreas	Worry
Stomach	Nervous
Thyroid, Adrenals	Paranoia

Reference: Professional Complementary Health Formulas, Oregon Homotoxicology Energetix International College of BioEnergetic Medicine, 2006

ADDITIONAL TESTIMONIES

WHIPLASH

Fifteen years ago, a woman received whiplash from an auto accident, which caused pain in her neck and frequent migraines.

When she pictured Jesus with her at the accident, she was able to feel comfort, release the fear, and forgive the other driver. She said the pain was gone, but she still felt stiffness in her neck. When she pictured the accident again, she saw herself lying on the car seat motionless, in fear of being paralyzed. When she released this additional fear, the pain and stiffness left. She became aware that her neck misaligned in a way she previously did not recognize. We prayed over her neck and brainstem five times, and each time we prayed, the neck increased alignment and the pain dissipated. When I called her three days later, she reported there was still no pain or migraines.

BACK PAIN

After an injury, a man experienced a low-grade ache for fifteen years. He realized that the constant pressure he felt to work and not relax had aggravated his back even more. God took him back to a memory of when he was eleven years old. He experienced feelings of disappointment because he never seemed to be able to please or get approval from his father. This created a pressure to perform and a sense of sadness that had been with him ever since that day. After he pictured Jesus standing in front of him, protecting him from the rejection, he was able to let go of the sadness and forgive his father. I had the man cross his arms and picture Jesus giving that little boy a big hug. This made the man feel loved and accepted. The back pain, pressure, and sadness disappeared without us having to pray again.

BRONCHITIS

A woman told me she was diagnosed with bronchitis two months prior and had been admitted to the hospital for "blowing out her lung" from a severe cough. Even with various treatments, including the use of antibiotics, steroids, and inhalers, she had experienced only minimal improvement. She complained of a cough, difficulty breathing, tightness in her throat, and difficulty swallowing, which had begun started six months prior. When I asked what happened in her life six months ago, she said a family member died. After she pictured Jesus with her during the time of the loss, she released deep sadness and grief, which are frequent emotional causes of chronic lung conditions. When we prayed a brief prayer for God to bring healing, the woman was able to take full breaths and said she felt better.

PAINFUL THROAT AND DIFFICULTY SWALLOWING

A woman complained of tightness in her throat, and difficulty swallowing. When I asked what was currently happening in her life, she said her husband was not working and she found it diffi-cult to say anything to him. When I asked her to remember when she first had difficulty expressing her feelings, she remembered being a little girl and feeling that she had no voice and could not say anything. She felt worse when her parents were fighting. When she pictured Jesus protecting her from her parents' fighting, she was able to release the hurt, sadness, and fear of feeling helpless and not being able express herself. When we prayed for her throat to clear, she said the tightness was gone and she had no more dif-ficulty swallowing.

FIBROMYALGIA

A woman had fibromyalgia for ten years, which caused pain throughout her body at a level of eight. When God took her to a memory of being six years old and falling into a pool and sink-ing to the bottom because she could not swim, she became fearful, believing she was going to die. After another child grabbed her and held her head above the water, she could see her mother ignor-ing and rejecting her. This created years of hurtful and angry feel-ings toward her mother, which she held inside. When she pictured Jesus holding her and having fun together in the pool, she was able to let go of her hurt and anger, and forgive her mother. At that point, the pain in her body disappeared.

5

EMOTIONAL CONNECTIONS TO MIND ILLNESS

A forty-five-year-old woman named Sarah wanted prayer for a lifetime of intense anxiety, panic attacks, and a severely racing mind. The sense of fear she experienced was so debilitating throughout her life that she was unable to finish school, work, be in crowds, go outside, or concentrate on conversations. God revealed a early childhood memory of witnessing a parent's death, and then subsequent family deaths throughout her life, which formed the basis for her multiple mind symptoms. As a result, Sarah was diagnosed and treated specifically for the symptoms of panic and anxiety disorder, agoraphobia, claustrophobia, and attention deficit disorder (ADD), with minimal symptom relief—and no identification or treatment for her original emotional trauma. Before I prayed, I asked Sarah to imagine Jesus touching her head, as I placed my hand gently on her head, with her permission. I used the Steps for Healing Prayer as she imagined Jesus healing her mental health issues. After I cursed her emotional, visual, and memory trauma, Sarah was able to walk away with no anxiety and a clear mind!

Having someone like Sarah come to you and ask for prayer may feel intimidating, and seem like a daunting task due to the complex psychological issues that may be difficult to identify or release. Since the church historically does not normally address emotional healing, and there is little training available, this lack of knowledge creates fearful hesitation to pray for a person with mind (soul) illness issues. As a result, soul issues are not being identified, which contributes to blocked healing and a feeling of disappointment for everyone involved when healing does not happen. In these scenarios, there can be too much emphasis placed on incorrect causes, such as lack of faith, demonic attack, or sin, which only makes the afflicted person feel worse. These misconceptions about the lack of healing stem from a misunderstanding of the severity of trauma and the healing of soul issues. The good news is, God created your emotions and He has the same power and authority for healing emotional illness as He does for physical illness. And God gives you the power and authority when you pray for *all* illnesses. No matter what happens when you pray, just continue to pray. The more you seek God and pray for the people He brings to you, the more He will reward you. (See Hebrews 11:6.)

As I mentioned earlier, how your parents or early caregivers treated you translates into the formation of your belief system, and how you now feel about yourself. The Bible says your parents are to train you up in the way you should go, so that when you are older, you will not depart from it. (See Proverbs 22:6.) As a result, the level of attitude, affirmation, acceptance, availability, and affection you received is going to factor into how you feel and believe about yourself, and your acceptance of healing. If someone wants prayer who has a lot of depression and anxiety, but they cannot identify a time in their past when something bad happened to them, that is evidence of suppressed trauma or long-term systemic trauma as a way of life. There also may be chemical imbalance that will require prayer for God to rebalance the brain.

For example, you may remember a time when your parents yelled at you, which you describe as scary. You can go back to that one event to identify the emotion to release and restore the soul from that trauma. However, if your parents had a habit of yelling all the time, you may not identify the yelling or emotions as a problem, because it was part of living in the home and became normalized behavior. As a result, you would typically not identify hurt or feelings of fear as something unusual, and you would not be able to identify any wrong behaviors in your childhood. This type of constant negative emotion can be more devastating, because the effects of how you are treated go deeper into the core of your belief system and identity. In such cases, simply ask the afflicted person to picture themselves as a child, standing in their home, and ask them to describe what it was like for that child to grow up with their parents in that home. Next, help them release what they felt.

HEALING MIND CONDITIONS

Stressful experiences, especially in childhood, create imprinted memories, and, in turn, create within you certain methods of coping with your problems that become the routine for how you handle stress later in life.[17] Your experiences early in life create a baseline for how you think, feel, and act for the rest of your life, especially during stressful situations. In addition, since emotion has a significant amount of power over your physical body, it is a major reason why emotions must be addressed when physical healing is being blocked.

When healing doesn't happen, it is important to reveal and release early negative emotion that is blocking the healing, in order for God to replace it with His love and healing. What the prayee says about the pain in their life, especially from their childhood, is very important. The images and words they use, the volume of their voice, and their body language are all important factors for identifying when and where the trauma took place. (See chapter 12, Expanding Your Search When Healing Doesn't Occur.)

Since mental illness can be casued by genetic factors, conditions during pregnancy, changes in brain chemicals, and life

---

17. Kenneth R. Pelletier, *Mind as Healer, Mind as Slayer* (New York: Delta Book, 1977), 117.

situations,[18] be alert to any evidence that may indicate the origin of the condition. Listen to what the Holy Spirit tells you, and to the words of the person asking for prayer. Ask them if they are aware of when the emotional condition started. Next, I recommend you simply pray and command the mental illness or emotion to leave, in Jesus's name, or you can use the Steps for Healing Prayer. You can also ask some of the following questions to determine the origin of the emotion:

+ When did your emotional condition begin?

+ Describe your years growing up—were you depressed, unloved, or anxious? Did you feel empty or otherwise unhappy?

+ Do other family members have emotional or mental illness conditions?

+ When your mother was pregnant with you, was she experiencing any abuse, fear, depression, etc.?

+ Were you conceived before marriage? Did you feel wanted as a child?

MIND CONDITION TESTIMONIES

The following testimonies deal with only a few of the mind conditions that are more common. I recommend you use the Steps for Healing Prayer in such cases for revealing the lie, releasing the original trauma, and restoring the truth.

Anxiety Disorders, Panic Attacks—when there are general feelings of anxiety experienced for no reason, or during stressful or uncomfortable events, use the Steps for Healing Prayer starting with Step II in order for God to take the afflicted person to the point in their life when the feelings began to identify the original trauma. If the original trauma cannot be identified, that is often an

---

18. "Mental Illness," Mayo Clinic, October 13, 2015, http://www.mayoclinic.org/diseases-conditions/mental-illness/basics/causes/con-20033813 (accessed May 21, 2018).

indication the anxiety started earlier in life, perhaps as the result of living in a home with anxious caregivers.

There was a man named Bill who battled constant feelings of anxiety throughout his life, especially as an adult when there was any form of conflict. Because he had recently experienced a conflict with some church members, he was experiencing a higher level of anxiety than usual. He realized that his history of lacking confidence to deal with these situations had created a belief that God was unable to answer his prayers. Bill said he was feeling the anxiety in his chest and stomach at a level of eight. God took him back to a time when he was three years old and in the hospital for surgery. His parents left the room for an unknown reason. As a three-year-old, being left alone in a strange place, even for a short time, can create extreme feelings of terror and abandonment. Eventually, his parents returned to the room, but for the rest of his life, Bill carried the fear of being abandoned. I asked him to imagine Jesus coming into the hospital room while the boy was alone. Bill pictured Jesus holding him as I commanded the emotional trauma and any emotional spirits of abandonment, rejection, and terror to leave. I declared the love, light, life, comfort, and peace of Jesus to be present. As Bill felt safe to release the past emotion, the anxiety left and never returned.

Fears—when you identify fears, such as the fear of flying, crowds, conflict, being sick, etc., it is typically an indication of an earlier trauma that needs to be released. The fear the afflicted person describes may or may not be what they were originally afraid of. For example, one of the most common fears is a fear of conflict, which most often is related to childhood memories of hearing and seeing trauma. This includes living in homes with parents yelling and arguing, or frightful situations in childhood. I recommend you use the Steps for Healing Prayer for revealing and releasing the original trauma and restoring the truth.

A man had general anxiety and developed an intense fear of flying after a plane he flew in was hit by lightening five years prior. In the years since, prayer did not relieve his anxiety, which he described at a level five. After we asked God to heal the trauma of the plane incident three times, the feelings of anxiety would not dissipate. This was an indication of earlier trauma. God took the man to a memory of his mother, who had general anxiety because of her medical issues. The mother was fearful and overprotective, showing anxiety about everything. Using the Steps for Healing Prayer, the man pictured Jesus protecting him as a little boy. At that point, he was able to release the childhood fear and realize that it was his mother's fears that drove him, and not his own. The man was then able to release any additional fear related to the plane incident and, afterward, reported having no fear of flying.

Depression—this includes feeling sad, gloomy, and unmotivated, and often involves sleep disorders and persistent moodiness and/or apathy. If the afflicted person wants prayer for depression, have them describe the symptoms of depression and use the Steps for Healing Prayer, starting with Step II, in order for God to reveal when this feeling started, to release what was traumatic. Since depression symptoms can be related to a chemical imbalance, also pray for God to rebalance the mind.

Obsessive Compulsive Disorder (OCD)—this can include repetitive rituals or thoughts, unwanted ideas or impulses that repeatedly come to mind, or the need to complete certain actions, such as handwashing, counting, checking, hoarding, or arranging, in order to reduce anxiety symptoms. When a person has OCD, I ask them to imagine themselves standing in the doorway looking at a messy home. How would they feel if they were not allowed to make things clean or tidy? Typically, the person will say they feel out of control, anxious, overwhelmed, frustrated, or under pressure. At that point, I use the Steps for Healing Prayer, starting with Step II, in order for God to take the person to the time when the OCD started, and to release any similar emotion from the past that may have created the unhealthy adult condition.

Anger—this can include outbursts, road rage, irritation, adult temper tantrums (slamming doors, punching walls, throwing things, silent treatment), inappropriate expression of words or behaviors, etc. Ask the person to think of a current situation that made them angry. Use the Steps for Healing Prayer, starting with Step II, in order for God to take them to a time when this feeling began, and to release any past emotion that may have created the adult condition.

Unworthiness—general belief of not being good enough, unloved, unattractive, stupid, etc. Ask the afflicted person what it feels like when they experience these beliefs. Use the Steps for Healing Prayer, starting with Step II, in order for God to take them back to a time when these feelings started, to release any past emotion that may have created the adult condition.

ACTIVE LISTENING

Hurting people will feel more encouraged to express their feelings when they feel safe and comforted through the following process of active listening:

- Show your interest—look at the person's face as you listen to their story.

- Gentle touch—if appropriate, touch the person's shoulder, upper arm, or back area to show compassion and encouragement.

- Validate the emotion—repeat what you heard, or comment on the emotion you see on the person's face. Use simple statements, such as, "It sounds like you were scared when...," or "you seem really sad about...."

- Using their emotion as an entry point to healing as you validate the afflicted person, ask them if they are ready to become free from these emotions. You may begin using the Steps for Healing Prayer.

HOW TO CALM SOMEONE OVERWHELMED WITH EMOTION

The goal with healing prayer is to allow Jesus to heal the illness, not to repeat all the details of the trauma. However, when the afflicted person is overwhelmed with emotion, ask them to imagine Jesus (or another trusted person) standing beside them, making it a safe environment for releasing the past emotion. The following is a list of do's and don'ts to help the person through their emotions.

DO'S:

+ Use active listening, as mentioned above, with the addition of making reassuring comments, such as, "You're doing great letting it out," "You're in a safe place to share your feelings," or "You're going to be okay; these are old feelings that are finally coming out."

+ Be mindful of other hindrances that may be surfacing, such as guilt, fear, sin, and spiritual warfare, all of which can create more emotion.

+ Have the person keep their eyes open and reassure them that they are in a safe place to share their feelings. As their feelings from past trauma are released, reassure them again, using statements such as, "These are emotions from past hurts," "It's time to let them out," and "You are in a safe place now."

DON'T'S:

+ Do not automatically assume the release of excessive emotion is sin, spiritual attack, or a way to sabotage your efforts.

+ Do not take what the person says personally—doing so only confirms your own soul issues.

+ Do not become fearful and overwhelmed that you will fail or won't know the right thing to say.

+ Do not yell or raise your voice, as if you are having to become more powerful. This can make the afflicted person feel afraid or upset, and lose their trust in you.

+ Do not tell the person that they have a lack of faith, demonic issues, or a sin problem.

Excessive amounts of emotion, such as hysterical crying or sobbing, are often the release of old trauma and emotional pain, rather than a symptom of demonic spirits. (You still have the option to use spiritual warfare prayers in case there actually *are* demonic spirits to release.) When these trauma emotions surface, continue reassuring the person by having them imagine Jesus protecting them by standing between the prayee and the trauma. In conclusion, use the following steps to help someone with overwhelming emotion.

1. Reassure the person with active listening and validation.

2. Remember the Do's and Don'ts list.

3. At eye level, sit in front of the afflicted person. If they are in a hysterical state, make sure they look at you. Say things like, "Look at me. Listen to what I'm saying. I hear you are really afraid right now, but you are in _(your location)_ talking to me. The person you are afraid of is not here. Look where you are. You are safe right now. Repeat after me, 'I am at _(your location)_ . I'm not with with that person. I am safe.'" Refer back to the image of Jesus being with them as they continue the Steps for Healing Prayer.

4. If the afflicted person becomes worse, or if you detect spiritual warfare, you have the option of binding and commanding any demonic spirit to leave, breaking off generational curses, or rebuking evil strongholds and declaring peace and the blood of Jesus over the person.

(See chapter 10 for suggested prayers.) You may refer to the book *Finding Victory When Healing Doesn't Happen*, and read the section entitled Spiritual Warfare for more details on how to identify and pray for demonic spirits.

CHOOSING HEALING WITH EMOTIONAL RELEASE AND/OR SPIRITUAL WARFARE PRAYERS

As you read in chapter 2, when a physically or emotionally unhealthy event occurs, emotional trauma will create a weakened condition in the body and mind. From a spiritual point of view, the longer you live in this unhealthy condition, the greater the opportunity evil spirits have to take advantage of your weakened state by attaching to the trauma, making your pain and suffering worse.

Evil spirits are always looking for a way to attack (see John 10:10), and trauma can be a door that allows the evil spirit to enter if you do not obtain healing for the trauma. When you release the pain of emotional and physical trauma, you decrease the chances of additional torment from evil spirits attaching to that trauma, and you close the door to evil taking advantage of you. More importantly, if you are a believer in Jesus Christ, you are already set free (see Galatians 5:1) from evil and darkness (see Colossians 1:13), because Jesus is the way, truth, and the life from death and sin (see John 14:6). This means you are already set free from evil spirits, filled with His spirit (see 1 Corinthians 3:16), and protected from harm—unless the door is opened due to trauma and the emotion from that trauma is held inside. I am not saying you will be influenced by evil spirits any time you experience trauma. However, the longer you hold on to unhealthy emotions, the greater the opportunity for some type of attack.

Since the church does not traditionally address emotions in healing prayer, most prayer ministers do not ask deep enough questions—something I like to call "expanding the search"—to uncover the original event that created the trauma. As a result, if healing does not happen and the physical condition persists, demonic spirits are often treated as the focal point, rather than taking the time to reveal the original traumatic issues that allowed the spirits in. Consequently, when emotional trauma is the original problem and primary barrier, if you begin the healing process with demonic warfare prayers, you may feel some relief and freedom, but not experience full release of the unhealthy emotional issues. As a result, demonic spirits can return, reattach themselves to the emotion, and make the condition worse.

It is important to reveal and release the original trauma, forgive the offender, and replace the hurt with Jesus's love, which closes the trauma door and restores your soul back to its original state of freedom. If the evil spirit attaches itself to the emotion of the physical trauma, that spirit can root itself and spread into other areas of your life. Remember, if you are a believer, you already have all the power and authority of Jesus. (See Acts 1:8; Colossians 2:9–11.) So, when you release the emotional root, the evil spirit will often automatically fall away, because it has nothing on which to attach itself. However, if you hold on to the unhealthy emotion and the spirit is allowed to take root and spread, you may also need to use your authority in Jesus to command any evil spirits to leave. (See chapter 10 for prayers.)

Tony asked me to pray for his anxiety, insecurity, confusion, and dread, which he had experienced for many years of his life. However, these feelings had grown worse ever since he received deliverance ministry. Tony was told he had a controlling spirit that was causing anxiety and torment within him. After Tony described his feelings of fear and dread, it confirmed my original thought, that although there was a spiritual attachment to this torment, his aforementioned issues were originating from unresolved past emotional trauma and not from a spiritual issue such as the demonic. I could tell it was more emotionally based, because his descriptive words were similar to those of a helpless child, and the ministry he received did not deal with the emotion.

Sensing he had more fear about his own spiritual well-being, especially the fact that he might be possessed, I immediately reassured him that his issues were based on unresolved emotions, not necessarily demon possession. When we prayed and used the Steps for Healing Prayer, God immediately took Tony back to his childhood and a father who was controlling and abusive. When he felt protected by picturing Jesus standing in front of him as a little boy, he was able to recognize the source of his fears and forgive his father. Immediately, the sense of dread and torment released and he felt total freedom. Tony finally realized the sense of torment was the accumulation of feelings experienced throughout childhood, and that the evil spirit had only made his dread worse.

I have routinely found that entering into healing prayer by revealing the sin and/or emotion from the original trauma has been successful in attaining permanent release, and restoring the body and soul with little to no demonic interference. However, if an evil spirit does show itself, you have the authority in Jesus to tell it to leave. Once you release the sin, emotion, or negative beliefs, the demonic forces do not have a foothold or reason to become attached. You can reclaim your inheritance as a Christian who is set free because of what Jesus has done for you. This direct approach is effective for quick resolution of the original problems, and increases the opportunity of a permanent healing outcome. I recommend your focus and words should primarily be about Jesus, and, if necessary, that you would use His authority to command anything evil to leave. As a result, this will not give evil the opportunity to gain any rights over anyone, or anything, to whom you are ministering.

6

WHEN THERE IS NO REASON FOR THE ILLNESS OR CONDITION

A man came to me who had been worried for six weeks about an uncomfortable lump in his throat. He said it felt like a cottonball was stuck in it. A medical examination could not determine the cause. He denied that he had experienced any particular stress at the time when the lump started. When I mentioned that the emotional origin was often due to the feeling that you do not have a voice, the Holy Spirit took him to a past memory in which he had been hurt and angry when he was not hired for a job he had applied for. When he released his anger, his throat discomfort decreased by half. He then remembered feeling angry and helpless when he could not say or do anything about an incident during childhood. When he pictured Jesus standing between him and his parents, the man felt protected by Jesus and was able to release the anger and forgive his parents. The feeling of having a lump in his throat disappeared with a simple prayer.

Like this man, if you ignore your feelings regarding life circumstances, you will become so accustomed to unhealthy feelings, you will not recognize they exist or why you feel the way you do. However, your mind and body will continue to send messages about unhealthy emotions that are causing your unhealthy physical conditions. As previously mentioned, when you have been holding an emotion in long enough, it will settle in the body organ or area experiencing a weakened condition. This creates a state of disharmony in that body area, which can become a state of disease or illness.

Traditional medical treatment that focuses primarily on the physical or mental symptoms as the primary problem source may have little success for permanent healing when there is no treatment of the suppressed, unresolved emotion from the original trauma. The longer traditional healing attempts are unsuccessful, the greater potential there is for establishing doubt that healing is possible. As a result, you have a shift in thought, attitude, and behavior, because the condition consumes your life and you feel there are no other options. In order to live with the long-term condition, your identity and daily life patterns adapt to the symptoms, which slowly incorporates the condition into your identity. You adapt to the condition as a way to cope and survive with a terrible situation that you have no control over.

When I ask someone suffering from a long-term physical condition to share about his or her emotional pains, they often do not see the emotional connection to the illness, and hence, they believe they must continue to suffer with their condition. One of the reasons for this book is to provide answers for desperate people who do not know why they have an illness or symptom and why it is not being healed.

INDICATORS THAT EMOTIONS ARE BARRIERS TO HEALING

When healing does not occur, the following conditions of the mind and body (excerpted from the book *Finding Victory When Healing Doesn't Happen*) are indicators that emotions may be barriers to healing:

+ Injuries causing pain and discomfort that come and go for little or no known reason.

+ Aches and pains that appear for no known reason, and any pain and discomfort that come and go for little or no known reason.

+ Long-term chronic conditions that do not improve with a variety of treatment modalities; (other causes for chronic conditions can include conditions such as reactions to medication, food allergies, and food additives, plus environmental issues such as electric fields, magnetic fields and radio frequencies, cellphones, WiFi, mold, etc.).[19]

+ When there is a feeling of being wronged, or an injury caused by someone or some entity, including church, workplace, or school (most evident with indicator statements about unfairness, being unjustly wronged, anger, hurt, a desire to get even, or unforgiveness).

+ When emotional reactions or the description about the condition are verbalized as if the incident happened a week ago, when in fact it occurred a year or more ago.

+ When there is a personal history of physical, mental, emotional, sexual, spiritual, and financial abuse, or the witnessing of traumatic events such as a house fire, accident, military service trauma, and the loss of an emotionally close relative or pet.

+ When experiencing long-term stressful and/or traumatic situations related to medical, physical, financial, occupational, or emotional situations.

If any of the aforementioned indicators are present, pray for the Holy Spirit to reveal to the afflicted person what emotional and physical problems need to be healed first. Next, use the Steps for Healing Prayer with what is revealed. For some people, the aforementioned indicators may not be seen as a problem, and they may believe they have "worked through" their trauma, especially if they have gone through forgiveness steps or attended a healing seminar. Although some healing may have occurred, people typically do not take the time, or have the expertise and opportunity to work through the multiple layers of emotion. In addition,

---

19. For more information regarding environmental and electronic hindrances, go to www.createhealthyhomes.com.

the more traumatic the event, and the longer emotions have been suppressed, the more they will normalize how they feel, which only makes it more difficult to identify the emotions and trauma. Typically, when the person has a quick response, such as, "Yeah, I've dealt with that" or "I've forgiven them," and there is no reference to experiencing an emotional release, it is less likely the emotion has been released at a deeper level. I recommend you tell the afflicted person, "No matter what ministry you have had in the past, be open to where God takes you, as if you have never experienced healing prayer." Then begin praying for the Holy Spirit to reveal emotional or physical problems. (This is to be used with the Steps for Healing Prayer.)

One important note is that if the traumatic situation or emotion appears to be greater than the knowledge and expertise of the prayer minister, or if it is more than the afflicted person wants to divulge, I recommend the person be referred to a healing ministry or Christian counselor to reveal and release deeper issues.

OTHER CAUSES OF SUPPRESSED EMOTION

The following is a list of additional influences that can cause the suppression of emotion in ways that you may not realize. When these influences are in your life, you may have an increased difficulty to receive healing.

+ Diet: Foods such as sugar and salt can cause moodiness, depression, anxiety, and other disorders.

+ Depression: Symptoms of depression may include sadness, suppressed emotion, isolation, social withdrawl, poor or excessive diet habits and sleep patterns, severe moodiness, thoughts of suicide, or hyper/manic thinking.

+ Medication: Side effects from medication may cause moodiness, anxiety, drowsiness, and changes in diet and sleep habits.

+ Sleep deprivation: Lack of sleep can cause symptons such as impaired judgment, poor concentration and communication skills, slower reaction times, forgetfulness, and a low threshold to express negative emotion.

+ Attention deficit disorder (ADD): Symptoms may include difficulty expressing feelings, poor attention span, prone to distraction, inability to focus on a conversation, and poor communication.

+ Religion: Any faith tradition that discourages the expression of emotions.

+ Personality disorders: Unemotional, or emotionally stuck, personality or way of life.

+ Home environment: Living with a spouse, parents, or siblings who are unemotional and/or discourage the healthy expression of emotions.

+ Domestic violence: Increases the stress level, anxiety, and depression. (See chapter 10, "Practical Tips for Breaking Through to Healing," for more details about domestic violence.)

7

SPIRIT, SOUL, BODY, AND HEALING

SPIRIT/SOUL/BODY CIRCLE

As a person of faith who knows Jesus in your heart, you have three parts: spirit, soul, and body. (See 1 Thessalonians 5:23.) Throughout your life, you should continually be growing by renewing your thoughts and actions (see Romans 12:1–2), toward the goal of becoming more like Christ. Each part is important in the healing process. I will explain each one.

SPIRIT

When you accept Jesus in your heart, your life should be about living through the Spirit of God. Your spirit is the center, or core, of your being, the life-giving part of you. (See James 2:26.) Your spirit cannot be seen or felt, and it is completely surrounded by your soul. When you pray in your spirit, and you think and feel the prayer through your mind and heart (your soul), you are aligning your soul and spirit to experience life in the presence of God. This means when you pray from the spirit for God to heal, you are aligning your soul with the supernatural life power and authority of the spirit, in order to connect with the body.

SOUL

The soul is made up of three parts: mind, will, and emotion. Your beliefs and emotions come through your soul. Even Jesus expressed His emotions in statements such as, "*My soul is deeply grieved, to the point of death*" (Matthew 26:38) and "*My soul has become troubled*" (John 12:27).

God has given you a mind with a free will. Out of love and respect for you, God will not take away something He gave you as a gift. Whenever you are hurt, you are able to choose what to do with the emotions you carry inside. You can choose how to express your feelings, how to feel about yourself, and what to believe about God's authority and promise to heal. Consequently, all of these choices impact whether you are healed or remain in your illness. But if you are also carrying emotional trauma that is contributing to the cause of your physical condition, God can heal the trauma. If you are not ready to reveal and release the various layers of emotion, He will allow you to continue to carry it and it will become a barrier to your healing. I have experienced God healing everything all at once, with a very simple prayer. And at other times, conditions are only healed as each layer is released.

As an emotional person, if you can hold on to soul hurts long enough, they can become part of your identify. However, God wants you to be free, and to never stop asking Him to reveal and release whatever is blocking your healing. This is also why you can feel God's love and joy in your spirit, while at the same time carry around unresolved trauma and sickness. (See Galatians 5:22.) Since your prayer from the spirit should be aligned with the soul, your healing prayers can be hindered if the soul (your mind, will, and emotion) is filled with unresolved issues.

When I saw a friend with an arm cast, I asked if I could pray with her. She shared her extreme disappointment about falling on her arm while on vacation. She had fractured her wrist and felt a constant pain at a level of nine. I asked God for healing of the fracture and rebuked the pain, which lowered the pain to a level five. When we prayed a few more times, the pain would not go lower than a level four. We had to stop praying at that time, so I told her that God heard our prayers and told her to be persistent about her belief in healing. She told me that, through the night, she consistently believed God would take away the pain, and as she continued to maintain her thinking that pain had no authority in her life, she became pain free. She had another X-ray within a few days, and the doctors said they could not find the fracture. She was completely healed.

BODY

The body is not specifically referring to your physical body, but more generally refers to how you relate to the world through the five natural senses of touch, smell, taste, sight, and hearing. Worldly thinking (secular or scientific perspective) can view the results of prayer by your ability, knowledge, facts, and five senses, to determine the outcome of the prayers. This limits your belief to only what is logical, using only your eyes and nerve endings rather than using your faith in the unseen. (See 2 Corinthians 4:18.)

Kingdom thinking is when you view healing out of the spiritual nature, by focusing on what Jesus would do rather than on what only you can do. This is why, when you rely on facts and what you see, you are not using your faith. Faith is about believing something that is impossible for you, but is very possible for God. For example, since your conditions and internal beliefs do not determine the reality of God's power, kingdom thinking is believing in the unseen and living by faith rather than by what you see or feel in the natural. Jesus lived in the world, but did not define His reality by the world. His reality is living in the infinite, unseen heavenly realm, where nothing is impossible. (See Luke 1:37.) In essence, when you believe like Jesus, you will live by faith, and pray believing the impossible is possible.

At the grocery store, a woman in front of me was walking with severe limp. I asked her if she had pain in her leg. She said her left knee had become worse over the last year, with pain at a level seven. She had already had both shoulders and her right knee replaced, so she did not want to have surgery again. I told her I have prayed for people with knee pain and God took their pain away. She responded, "Really? Wow." I asked if I could pray for her knee. She responded, "Sure." I put my hand on her shoulder, and said, "God, You love this woman, and she doesn't want to have surgery. You would prefer her to depend on You. So right now, I bind the arthritis and send away the spirit of pain. Heal her and grow cartilage in her knee."

I then asked what she felt. She said she only felt pain when she walked. I asked her to thank Jesus for her healing, and to take a few steps in faith. She walked with a smile on her face. Her pain was now at a level four. Again, I said a simple prayer for God to bring more healing, and for the pain to leave. Then I asked her to walk again. The pain was now at level two. One more time, I said a short, one-sentence prayer for the pain to leave and for more healing. She was amazed. "Wow," she exclaimed. "I don't feel any pain at all." I told her that it was because God loved her. I thanked God and instructed her about how to keep her healing. (More about that in chapter 14.) The more you encourage people to "practice" their healing by stepping out in faith, the more God will reward them with healing, and the more they will have faith to keep their healing.

HOLDING ON TO YOUR EMOTIONS

God hears your prayers. He can heal anyone at anytime, and He wants you to be healed. However, God also created your mind, will, and emotions (your soul) and gave you freedom of choice in how to deal with your emotions. He will allow you to keep unhealthy emotions if that is your choice. You will hear people say they want healing, but they do not realize their unconscious need to hold on to unhealthy emotion, especially if it meets a need or is how they learned to live life. For example, you may not recognize your defensive responses, hear your angry tone, or feel your fear of conflict, especially if these behaviors have been part of you since childhood. With the Steps for Healing Prayer, you can reveal and release unhealthy soul issues.

GOD WANTS YOU HEALED

First of all, God loves you so much that He wants you to be fully healed, not just partially healed. Second, God knows your needs, and He is more aware of what you need to release. Third, God wants you to get to know Him personally, and He wants you to spend more time listening to Him than asking of Him. As a result, if healing doesn't happen, you can learn to expand your search for the emotional trauma that may be blocking your healing.

For twelve years, a woman had pain in her jaw (TMJ), tension and stiffness in her neck, and difficulty opening or closing her jaw. She experienced insomnia, headaches, and frequent migraines. Past prayer and various treatments were unable to relieve the pain, and to make matters worse, she also had emotional trauma from trying to end an abusive relationship.

When I asked what it was like to live this way, she said it was tense, scary, hurtful, and abusive. When we prayed for the Holy Spirit to reveal when she had felt like this before, God brought to her mind an image that represented the pain from her parents' abuse. I asked her to picture Jesus protecting her by standing between her and her parents. When she felt safe with Jesus, she was able to release the emotional trauma, physical trauma, and forgive her parents, making it possible to walk away completely pain free, with no tension and complete movement of her neck and jaw.

JESUS RELEASING EMOTIONS IN PRAYER

As a man, even Jesus expressed His emotions to bring healing. Just before He spent time praying at the garden of Gethsemane, Jesus told his disciples, *"My soul is deeply grieved, to the point of death"* (Matthew 26:38). It was only after Jesus released this extreme emotion of agony and intense fear that He was able to continue praying, *"My Father, if this cannot pass away unless I drink it, Your will be done"* (verse 42). We know how extreme the emotion was for Jesus during that time of prayer, since Luke the physician writes, *"And being in agony He was praying very fervently; and His sweat became like drops of blood, falling down upon the ground"* (Luke 22:44). The intense agony that caused Jesus to experience the sweating of blood is a medical condition called *hematidrosis*, in which the vessels release blood through the sweat glands under intense stress and agony. Since Jesus was experiencing human physical conditions, it would be difficult for anyone to make logical decisions during such an emotional time. It would seem understandable that it was not until Jesus released the extreme emotion that caused Him to sweat blood that He would be better able to make the decision to fulfill the will of His Father. You may not experience something as traumatic as Jesus did, but God also wants you to release unhealthy emotions to improve your ability to hear from Him to make healthier decisions in life.

FREE WILL TO EXPRESS EMOTIONS

Because God created you with a free will, you have the freedom to make your own decisions. The more you hold in unhealthy emotions, the more your emotions will overpower your ability to make logical decisions, and hinder you in believing in your own healing. Logic and emotion need to work together to create value and importance with balanced life decisions. For example, as an adult, if you experience intense anxiety whenever someone raises their voice, it may be evidence that you are functioning primarily from childlike emotions, rather than from an adult reaction involving your logic. This means your emotions (and not your logic) are the driving force in how you react to stressful situations. If you were using your logic, you would recognize that those people are in conflict or raising their voice out of their own immaturity issues, and you would logically realize there is less reason for fear. If you have a greater emotional reaction than is necessary for your current circumstances, that is evidence you are still living out of unresolved negative emotions within the soul nature. Often, these emotions are created earlier in life, and held inside until they become your normal reaction. Over time, these unhealthy emotions and beliefs can become so real, they are incorporated into your identity and into how you function.

How you align your thinking can determine your healing outcome. If you align your thinking between your soul and body, what you physically feel and see in the world, you will solely depend on your natural senses and be limited to those senses and beliefs to determine your healing. If, on the other hand, you align your thinking between your soul and spirit, you will have unlimited possibilities, because your belief in healing will align with what God can do, regardless of what or how you feel. (See Ephesians 1:3.) You will learn more about how to obtain what God wants you to have and how to reveal and release unhealthy emotions in the chapters to come.

8

WHY IT IS HARD TO BELIEVE IN YOUR AUTHORITY TO HEAL

In my earlier years of praying for healing, I did not realize how much I struggled with believing I had the authority of God to heal others. If someone asked for a simple prayer of encouragement for a sore throat, I would pray, hoping God would come through. However, if someone in a wheelchair came to me, I would experience some panic inside, and perhaps the sudden need to use the restroom or grab someone else to help me pray. I had a lack of self-assurance when someone asked me to pray. Even after I prayed, I would question whether I said or did the right thing. I knew this thinking was not correct, since the power and authority of Jesus was the same for a sore throat as it was for someone in a wheelchair, but I could not seem to shake my insecurity about whether God would actually work through my prayers.

Growing up in the church, I was told about God's wrath and love, but I was not told that when you accept Jesus in your heart, you receive the fullness of everything He has. (See John 1:16.) Many people do not realize that when Jesus died, your old nature died with Him and you became a *new creature*. (See 2 Corinthians 5:17.) Therefore, when you ask for forgiveness and accept Jesus in your heart, you are set free from your old sins. And as a new creature, you receive all of His spirit to *dwell* in you. (See 1 Corinthians 3:16.) That is amazing news. It means you have the same power and authority as Jesus does, in order to ask God to heal. However, if you struggle in your confidence to believe in God's authority, there is a bigger issue you must deal with. The issue is not with God; it is with your own struggle to believe. If you feel that you are not good enough, unworthy, doubting, unable to receive love, and struggling to believe in your authority to heal, you have a crisis of belief.

I was talking with an eighty-year-old man who had a strong faith. When I asked about receiving prayer, he told me he had a lot of doubt in himself and confessed that he did not have much confidence in praying for people, especially for his wife to be healed. He wanted me to pray for him to increase his belief to see God heal when he prayed. He continued to tell me how he felt sad and discouraged when he did not see change after he prayed. Since I discerned this man of faith should not be feeling this doubt, I asked God to take the man back in time when he felt doubt, poor confidence, and discouragement as a child. God showed him a memory as a five-year-old playing in a sandbox all alone. He remembered feeling discouraged and emotionally distant from his parents. I asked him to picture Jesus coming into the sandbox with him. In the name of Jesus, I commanded the emotional and physical trauma, loneliness, sadness, and discouragement to be gone. Then I prayed for Jesus to fill his heart with light, love, joy, and encouragement. The man immediately had a smile on his face as he saw Jesus giving him attention and playing with him. The man said he felt lighthearted, and he experienced a feeling of warmth coming over him. He then said, "I can't wait to go home to pray for my wife!"

YOU BELIEVE BECAUSE SOMEONE FIRST BELIEVED IN YOU

Your crisis in belief is created early in your life from some authority figure who did not believe in you. In essence, the amount and type of love you receive from important people early in your life can determine your measurement of worth and value for the rest of your life. In addition, the amount of worth you have determines your measurement of trust and faith, both in others and in God. For example, receiving words of affirmation, such as "good job," "I'm proud of you," and "I love you," as well as signs of affection, such as hugs and kisses, ultimately create your measurement of faith to believe in yourself and your healing. However, when you do not receive love, or when authority figures say negative comments early in life, your "love bank" will be empty and, later in life, you will be more prone to negative thoughts and opinions about life and your abilities. You will doubt, question, and struggle to believe you are worthy of healing.

Scripture lets you know that you love because God first loved you. (See 1 John 4:19.) Since you were born not knowing God, your earthly parents (especially your father) were your first role models of your heavenly Father's love, power, and authority. Unless you are shown differently, whatever you learned (or did not learn) from your parents will become ingrained in how you interpret, give, and receive love, power, and authority from your heavenly Father. As a result, your external experiences early in life determine your internal beliefs later in life, as the Scriptures state: *"Train up a child in the way he should go, even when he is old he will not depart from it"* (Proverbs 22:6). What you experience during the most influential time of life creates an imprint for the rest of your life, unless you resolve and release the unhealthy emotion and belief.

One night, there was a mother lying on the couch with a high fever. Her seven-year-old son asked if he could pray to make her better. As she agreed, the boy put his hand on her head and simply asked God to take the fever away. Before the next morning, the fever was gone and the mom was back to normal. The boy was accustomed to seeing the power of prayer practiced through his family, which created an unquestioning faith and belief that prayer would help his mom. In Mark 10:15, Jesus told the disciples to *"receive the kingdom of God like a child."* A child's faith can be simple enough to carry the power and authority to believe that God will do what you ask. It is often the case that the wounds of the soul can hinder the ability to pray and believe with childlike faith.

The love, praise, and acceptance received (or not received) early in life from your earthly authority figures will translate into the same love, praise, and acceptance with your heavenly authority figure. The following chart shows the correlation between what you are given early in life and how it is translated into what you will believe or feel later in life.

When you are	=	You will believe you are:
Loved (hugs/kisses)	=	Loved, good enough, worthy, deserving
Believed in	=	Confident, deserving of what God has for you
Encouraged	=	Encouraged, confident, able to step out, believe
Listened to	=	Heard, valued, important, cared for by God
Comforted	=	Comforted, reassured, at peace, loved

When you are:	=	You will believe you are:
Not loved/hugged	=	Not loved, not good enough, unworthy, undeserving
Criticized	=	Unconfident, unworthy, insignificant, unimportant
Not believed in	=	Doubtful, not believing self, limiting faith
Discouraged	=	Stuck/afraid of future, not confident, discouraged

Not listened to	=	Unheard, without a voice, unimportant
Not comforted	=	Worried/anxious, not loved or close to God
Ignored	=	Not believed, unimportant, insignificant, empty, lost

HOW YOUR PAST RELATES TO HEALING

When caregivers and authority figures early in life do not give you what you need as a child, you can struggle emotionally, spiritually, and physically later in life. The bullet point section that follows will give you examples of how you will struggle with your beliefs about healing when growing up with the following caregivers and/or people you lived with:

+ Caregivers and people who were emotionally or physically unavailable, broke promises, left the family, died, or divorced: your healing can be hindered by unhealthy feelings such as depression, distrust, and not hearing, feeling, or receiving love from God. You struggle to believe you are good enough, worthy enough, or deserving enough to receive healing or have anyone pray for your healing. You feel God is distant, has abandoned you, and cannot be trusted to be available when you pray.

+ Caregivers and people who were not comforting or affectionate, religiously strict, legalistic, judgmental, critical, abusive, or condemning: your healing can be hindered by interpreting God as critical, angry, judgmental, unloving, distant, and punitive. You feel unworthy and undeserving of God's comfort, approval, love, forgiveness, and healing. You do not have enough faith. You feel you must be perfect or you must work for God's love and healing.

+ Caregivers and people who were not good listeners or discounted your feelings and opinions: your healing can be hindered by believing your prayers, opinions, thoughts, feelings, and healing are not important, unheard, not valuable, unworthy, unwanted, and insignificant to God.

During healing prayer, if any of the above unhealthy feelings or beliefs are verbalized by the afflicted person, use the Steps for Healing Prayer to reveal the origin of these unhealthy feelings, and then release these feelings before you begin the process of restoring healthy feelings. It is often the case that healthy beliefs will automatically become recognized as a result of releasing unhealthy feelings.

HOW TO BELIEVE IN YOUR GOD-GIVEN AUTHORITY AND POWER

If your faith is struggling to believe in your spiritiual authority to pray for healing, the following are suggestions to increase your confidence to believe and minister with the authority and power of God.

+ Change wrong perceptions. Find the origin of your unbelief and lack of confidence by addressing the wounded soul issues. Do not let negative emotions and ungodly beliefs overrule the truth about your authority and healing. Negative words and beliefs are evidence of unresolved wounds and negative emotion somewhere in your past. Unresolved emotion is strong enough to override your belief in the truth of God's Word. Do the following steps to identify the negative emotion as you follow the Steps for Healing Prayer:

  – Think of authority figures, caregivers, important people, or events in your life that had a hurtful or negative impact on you. Think of the feelings you derived from each person or event that hurt you.

  – With each person (including God and yourself) or event, forgive them for what they did to you and made you feel. Ask God to bless them.

- Speak encouraging and uplifting words of life to yourself. For example, speak the positive words from the previous chart, "You will believe you are."

  Years ago, during healing prayer times, I would often struggle with what I was going to say when I prayed. I have come to realize I am only the vessel, allowing Jesus to operate through me. Now, I put the responsibility of healing on Jesus. When someone wants prayer, I ask in my spirit, *Jesus, what are You going to do and say through me for this situation?* If I do not hear anything, I can again pray aloud for the Holy Spirit to reveal truth, to myself or the person asking for prayer. As I ask the person more questions about their condition, I wait to see what the Holy Spirit reveals. I move forward in faith, believing in my God-given authority and knowing the Holy Spirit will meet our need. And He does.

✦ Create a closer relationship with Jesus to increase the belief in your authority. One of the best ways to believe in your authority is to spend more alone time with the One who gives you the authority. The more time you spend with Jesus, the more you will feel His acceptance and love. As a result, the more love you feel, the more you will believe you have the authority to use His authority. As with any relationship, the more time you spend together, the more you will grow together. Here are simple steps to feel closer to Jesus:

- Sit or lie in a comfortable place and pray the simple prayer, *Thank you, Holy Spirit, for Your presence, and for showing me the love of Jesus.* You can also pray whatever else God leads you to say.

- As you are relaxing, focus on Jesus being with you. Picture Jesus sitting next to you and ask Him for more of whatever He wants to give you. You can "soak" in His presnce, sitting or lying quietly or with soft, gentle music. Allow all your senses to be sensitive to your surroundings. Listen for His voice. *"Cease striving and know that I am God"* (Psalm 46:10).

+ Other helpful suggestions:

  – If a negative image comes to your mind, you can pray, *In Jesus's name, that negative thought is to go and never return. Holy Spirit, bring me an image of Jesus Christ.*

  – If your mind is racing and will not settle down, take a deep breath and ask Jesus to bring you peace. (You can use the Comfort and Revelation Step with the Love Hug, found in Step V, Soul and Spirit Restoration in the Steps for Healing Prayer.)

  – If your mind cannot settle down or relax because you are feeling overwhelmed, sad, or anxious, I recommend you use the Steps for Healing Prayer, or speak with a Christian prayer minister or professional to deal with emotional issues in your life.

+ If you do not experience positive change in the spiritual and emotional areas of your life:

  – Spend more time resting, and asking the Holy Spirit to tell you or take you where He wants you to go.

  – Seek a Christian counselor and/or an established healing ministry who works with the identification and release of soul wounds (mind, will, emotions, ungodly beliefs, sins, forgiveness) for inner healing.

  – Meditate on Scriptures about the authority, power, and the greater works that God will do through you. (For example, Matthew 10:1; Luke 9:1; John 14:12; Acts 1:8; Ephesians 1:3, 3:20; Philippians 4:13, 4:19.)

+ Remember these truths:

- Your heavenly Father is not the same as your earthly father.

- Your limited perceptions do not determine God's unlimited possibilities.

- Your internal beliefs do not determine the external reality of God's ability.

- Healing prayer is expecting the impossible because of God's authority working through you.

- It only takes one small tear to move the largest emotional mountain.

PART II
USING MIND-BODY CONNECTIONS
FOR HEALING

9

PRAYING FOR HEALING WITH POWER AND AUTHORITY

A man named Paul limped as he walked down the hall to bring his daughter for counseling. After we all sat down and introduced each other, I asked Paul why he was limping. He told me about his torn meniscus that had been getting worse over the past four months. Paul said he was currently having severe pain at around a number nine level. His doctors were recommending surgery, which Paul said he didn't want to have. I saw this as an opportunity to see God at work, so I asked if I could pray for his knee. After I received permission to place my hand on his knee, I asked God to release the emotional, physical, and cellular memory trauma and mend the torn meniscus. Paul said the knee was starting to get hot as his pain totally disappeared! Amazed, Paul started jumping up and down, saying, with the biggest smile, "Wow, I couldn't do this before." I explained that God loved him and wanted to bring healing to him and cared for the needs of his family.

A few months later, I saw Paul in the lobby waiting for a family member. I ask him about his leg when I saw him walk with a slight limp. He looked a little embarrassed as he said he had hurt his knee again while playing sports. He claimed it was not as bad as the last time we prayed, but he still had a pain level of number six and had difficulty walking. Once again, he agreed to pray, but this time, I wanted Paul to learn about his personal power and authority to heal. I asked him to point to his knee and issue a command with confidence: "I forgive myself for what I did. In the name of Jesus, I command the knee to be healed and the pain to go away." When I asked how much pain he felt now from zero to ten, he said it was at four. We praised God for His healing and I said, "Let's get rid of the rest of the pain." I asked him to command the pain to go away once more, in Jesus's name, believing the pain had no more authority to be a part of his body. After he commanded the healing with authority, the pain was gone and he walked away without any more difficulty.

YOU HAVE BEEN GIVEN POWER AND AUTHORITY

Just as Paul was able to command his knee to be healed, you also have the power and authority to command healing in your body.

Jesus did not die on the cross just for you to go to church and call it a day. When most people ask God for healing, there is a tinge of doubt in their request, as they wonder if it is really possible that God will break through their frailty and insecurity. Jesus, however, lived to be your example and died so you can pray with the same authority and power that He had. Remember, the reason you can pray with the same power and authority as Jesus is because Christ died for you, and now His Spirit dwells within you. (See 1 Corinthians 3:16.) When you accepted Jesus in your heart, you received everything Jesus has. (See John 1:16.) Consequently, as a Christian, you have the power over unclean spirits and the authority to heal every disease. (See Matthew 10:1; Luke 9:1.) The best part is that you can receive power in the same way that Jesus instructed His disciples in Acts 1:8: "*You will receive power when the Holy Spirit has come upon you.*" Simply ask for the Holy Spirit to fill your heart and you will receive more of His power! The next step is to pray with that authority.

PRAYING WITH POWER AND AUTHORITY

Since 20 percent of the Gospels are about the healing ministry of Jesus, it would seem logical that healing is one of the primary applications we are to learn from His ministry. What is interesting is that Jesus did not pray for healing in the traditional way we pray. In fact, He simply did not *pray* for God to heal people. He viewed infirmities and diseases as conditions that did not belong and had no legal right to exist as a part of the mind or body. As a result, He did not pray over people; instead, He took authority over the condition and firmly commanded it to leave. You are able to do the same. The following are suggestions to help you minister healing with authority and power.

1. Treat the condition, pain, or sensation as a foreign object that does not belong in the human body. Believe that you have full authority and power, in Jesus's name, and speak firmly with that full authority, commanding it to leave. For example, you can say, with confidence, "In the name of Jesus, I command the emotional, physical, and cellular trauma to leave. I command the pain to be gone and the torn muscle to be healed." (See Step II of the Steps for Healing Prayer.)

2. When you pray for healing, you have the option of using the words *command* or *curse*. I prefer to use the word *curse*, since Jesus cursed the fig tree so it wiould no longer bear fruit. (See Mark 11:21.) In addition, Adam and Eve used the fig leaf to hide their original sin. (See Genesis 3:7.) I want to use the same word that Jesus spoke to curse anything that has to do with the original sin, and in order to eradicate any trauma, sin, or negative thought from the person who is seeking healing.

3. Some people believe they are "intended" to experience pain as a normal condition of life. This way of thinking gives power to the pain and keeps the afflicted person in an unhealthy condition. Proverbs 23:7 states, "*As* [a man] *thinks within himself, so he is.*" In God's kingdom, you are to be healthy, not sick. Think of the pain as a foreign object

that has attached itself to you and has no legal right to be there. Curse the pain and tell it to leave in Jesus's name. If it returns, command it to leave again. If the pain continues, consider using Step II of the Steps for Healing Prayer.

4. Command the condition to leave with confidence, believing that what you are saying carries the authority of Jesus. If you begin to doubt, wonder, or question while you pray, you just allowed *your* mind to take control rather than the power of Jesus. As a result, more feelings of discouragement will appear if healing does not immediately occur. To get refocused, ask God to clear your mind of distraction; think of Jesus standing with you as you pray, and begin praying again with the authority of Christ central in your mind.

5. Use short, specific, confident commands. Often, but not always, the longer you pray, the more it becomes about you trying to *make* something happen out of your own insecurities. For example, the authority of a uniformed police officer only needs to tell you to stop once. When you use the authority of Jesus, your command automatically creates power and should not require many words.

STOP YOUR FAITH FROM BEING TESTED

If healing doesn't happen when you are ministering, your faith can be tested, and you may begin to experience doubt, feelings of inadequacy, and questions about your level of belief. Some of the common reasons for prayer ministers to question their faith are the following:

+ Unforgiveness, unrepentant sin, or other soul issues can hinder prayer and the ability to hear from God. This is especially true if you become emotionally triggered by the prayer concerns of others. As a result, it may be difficult to hear from God or remain objective when praying for others. If this occurs, spend your own time using Step II of the Steps for Healing Prayer, or ask another prayer minister to help you work through your soul issues.

+ Prayer ministers with good hearts can take on too much responsibility and disappointment over the prayer concerns and suffering of others. It is important to remember that it is not your responsibility to heal the person. Your obligation is to pray and believe for healing. God's obligation is to provide the healing. Give the condition to Jesus, no matter the outcome, and encourage the afflicted person to believe for their own healing. Taking on too much responsibility is a result of your own wounded heart. Spend time using Step II of the Steps for Healing Prayer in your own life, or ask another prayer minister to help you work through your soul issues.

10

STEPS FOR HEALING PRAYER

The Steps for Healing Prayer are utilized to pursue breakthough when healing does not happen. These steps are not to replace other prayer models you may have learned, nor are they designed to drag you through past trauma. These steps are used to reveal the original source of the trauma and safely release it, so permanent healing can occur. These prayers can be applied in person or remotely by phone to fully restore your life, or the life of the person you are praying for, with God's love, grace, and freedom. *For online demonstrations of these techniques go to: www.insightsfromtheheart.com.*

STEP I: PRAYER FOR HEALING

1. *Ask:* "What is your name? What do you need prayer for?"

2. *Ask:* "What is the amount [intensity level] you feel the condition in your mind/body?" (Use a pain scale of 0–10, with zero being no pain at all and ten being intense pain.)

3. *Command* the emotions, pain, and physical condition to leave, in Jesus's name.

4. *Ask:* "What is the amount [intensity level] you feel the condition now in your mind/body?" (Use the same 0–10 scale.)

5. *Praise* God for any healing. Repeat steps 1–5 for more healing.

6. *Instruct:* Teach the person how to believe for healing by focusing on God's Word, not on their pain or condition. Encourage them to give Jesus all their hurt.

If healing does not happen: *continue to Step II.*

STEP II: PRAYERS FOR RELEASING TRAUMA

1. *Ask:* "When did you first remember experiencing this condition or feeling?"

1a. If memory/reason for condition is *known*…	1b. If memory/reason for condition is *unknown*…
Ask: "Describe what happened, and how it made you feel." Proceed to #2.	*Ask/Pray:* "Describe your feelings of living with the condition." Pray to recall early memories that produced similar feelings. Proceed to #2.

2. *Ask:* Thinking of the past memory, rate the amount of hurt you feel the mind/body condition. (0–10 scale)

3. *Instruct:* "Picture Jesus [or another safe person] in the memory standing between you and the offending person/situation protecting/hugging you [see Step V Love Hug below] or hugging you within a protective bubble."

4. *Pray:* In Jesus's name, curse the emotional, physical, sight, hearing, and cellular memory trauma.

5. *Pray:* Declare healing to the heart/mind/body, in Jesus's name.

6. *Ask:* Rate the amount of hurt in your mind/body now. (0–10 pain scale)

7. *Praise* God for any healing or expected healing.

If healing does not happen: *expand your search* [see chapter on Expanding Your Search] for earlier trauma issues and repeat 1–8, with the option to use Step V (Love Hug and love pat).

If healing happens: option to continue with Step III and Step IV.

8. *Instruct:* Teach the person how to believe for healing by focusing on God's Word, not on their condition. Encourage them to give Jesus all of their hurt.

HELPFUL SUGGESTIONS DURING PRAYER:

+ At any time, for faster and deeper trauma release, simultaneously use Step II with Step V (Love Hug).

+ The prayer minister should pray with eyes open, to observe the afflicted person.

+ The afflicted person should receive prayer with eyes closed, to focus on their inner healing (or keep eyes open if the person feels safer that way).

+ Thank the Holy Spirit for being present with His guidance and power.

  – Trust the leading of the Holy Spirit, not your method.

  – Stop praying when: a) the person is healed; b) the person wants to stop; c) the Holy Spirit tells you to stop

+ Pray for one illness/memory at a time, unless you are lead to pray for many memories in one prayer.

+ During the healing of a traumatic memory, if other memories come to the afflicted person's mind, tell the person that you will address the additional memories after you finish healing the current memory issues.

HELPFUL SUGGESTIONS AFTER PRAYER:

+ If healing does not happen, do not accuse the person of lacking faith or having sin. Continue by expanding your search and simultaneously using Step II with Step V.

- If healing does happen, continue with Step III and Step IV. End the session by reviewing instructions for "Keeping Your Healing" and sharing encouraging Scripture passages.

- If appropriate, ask if the person wants to know Jesus, the One who healed them. Pray with them to accept Jesus in their heart. (See John 3:16; Roman 3:23, 8:1, 10:9–10.)

The following techniques are for deeper release and mind-body healing and restoration:

For online demonstrations of these techniques go to: www.insights-fromtheheart.com

STEP III: RELEASING THE OFFENDER AND FALSE RESPONSIBILITY

When someone has been offended or abused by others, they may hold on to false responsibility and offenses, which can create unhealthy feelings of guilt, shame, humiliation, regret, self-judgment, etc. Listen for phrases like "I'm bad," "I'm always wrong," "I'm helpless," "I'm afraid," or "I just cannot forgive." A person who holds on to these issues will remain in emotional bondage and their physical healing will be blocked. No one should suffer because of hurtful actions or words from someone else. Freedom from this bondage is achieved when the offended person verbally releases themself from any offense and from taking on any false responsibility resulting from that offense.

INSTRUCTIONS

After the afflicted person "feels" healed (or close to healing), ask them to repeat these statements below. You can add, delete, and alter the statements as is appropriate for each circumstance.

The prayer minister will say to the afflicted person, "Picture Jesus [or any safe person] standing between you and the offender/situation. With Jesus [or any safe person] protecting you, say these words out loud, as if you were talking to the offender."

+ I didn't like what you did to me.

+ What you did to me was unfair.

+ You made me feel (hurt, sad, angry, helpless, etc.)

+ I realize that I now have choices.

+ I choose to give Jesus my feelings of hurt and pain.

+ It is not my responsibility to carry these feelings anymore.

+ I choose to not allow these feelings to have any more authority over me.

+ I choose to give what you did to me to Jesus; you have no more authority over my feelings.

+ I choose to forgive you, so you have no more control over my life.

+ I repent for taking on any false responsibility for this situation.

+ I choose to let go of trying to fix you or this situation.

+ I realize you did not know how to love me, which is not my fault.

+ Heavenly Father, I choose to receive Your love.

+ Heavenly Father, fill my heart with Your love in a way my (parents) couldn't.

+ Thank You, Jesus, for my freedom and my healing.

STEP IV: DETERMINING COMPLETION OF MEMORY HEALING

When the afflicted person "feels" healed of a past trauma memory, and before stopping the ministry session or moving on to another memory, use this technique to determine if the unhealthy emotion is fully released and the memory completely healed.

Instruction:

1. After the healing of each past memory, have the person picture the younger image of themselves in that memory.

2. The prayer minister should ask, "Now that you feel that memory is healed, when you think of the earlier image of you in that memory, what do you see on your face? A smile, a frown, or a flat look?"

   - 2a. **If it is a smile:** Ask the person, "When you think of yourself in that past memory, do you believe this statement is true or false: 'The situation is over and I can feel safe now in that memory'?"

     - **If they say the statement is true,** have them thank Jesus for their healing. This session can end or continue to another memory.

     - **If they say the statement is false, continue to #3 below.**

   - 2b. **If it is a frown or a flat look:** Ask them what they are still feeling in that memory. **Continue to #3 below.**

3. Repeat 1 through 7 of **Step II: Prayers for Releasing Trauma** simultaneously with **Step V: Releasing Trauma Love Hug.**

4. After you pray and the trauma is considered healed or diminished, repeat steps 1–3 above until the person imagines themselves with a smile and feels safe in that past memory.

If the person still cannot imagine a smile after several prayers, *expand your search* (see chapter 12, "Expanding Your Search When Healing Doesn't Occur") to a previous memory with similar feelings, then repeat steps 1–3 of this section.

HELPFUL SUGGESTION:

Even if the afflicted person does not believe the person in their earlier image can smile due to their past trauma, continue the steps described above, and place your belief in the fact that God can heal everything and bring a smile to their face. God does not want anyone to live a life with a frown or in sadness.

STEP V: THE LOVE HUG—THREE METHODS FOR SOUL/ SPIRIT RELEASE AND RESTORATION

In healing ministry, you will pray for people who are emotionally stuck, numb, blank, or unable to identify or release emotions and memories; people who feel disconnected between mind and body; people who cannot hear from God or feel disconnected from Him; and people who cannot feel love from God. All of these issues interrupt the soul/body/spirit connection, which blocks the ability to hear from, feel, and sense God. It blocks belief in the ability to be healed or in the authority to heal others. If healing does not progress or occur at all, this can be a discouraging time for both the afflicted person and the prayer minister.

As I described earlier, blocked emotions and memories usually indicate a person did not feel safe during traumatic events, which causes them to shut down the emotions and memory from that event. As a result, they will not allow anyone (including God) to access that event for inner healing. Since everyone desires to be comforted and safe, the best way to achieve comfort is through the act of being loved. Therefore, during ministry time, it is important to recreate a memory in which the afflicted person feels protected in order for them to feel that it is safe to release the original trauma. The safer the afflicted person feels, the greater the potential to break through the barriers, in order to reveal and release suppressed emotion and memory.

One of the best ways for the afflicted person to feel safe is to actually experience the feeling of love and comfort. This is achieved through a simple method called the "Love Hug," a proven and effective way to assist people in revealing and releasing deep trauma in order to restore vital pathways for receiving soul/body/ spirit restoration.

Let me explain how the Love Hug will assist with healing in the following way. Think of how you would comfort someone who is emotionally upset, or how you would comfort a crying baby. One of the best ways to comfort someone is by putting your arms around them and gently patting them on the back, as you calmly say reassuring words, such as, "Everything is going to be all right" or "It's okay to cry; it's going to work out." This simple act of physical touch calms the nerves and brings a sense of peace to the mind and body. We know that physical touch stimulates the brain to produce substances such as serotonin, endorphins, and other natural pain suppressors that work as "feel-good" chemicals to naturally calm the brain and body. For example, if you hug someone and gently give them a pat on the back, this stimulates the sensory nerve endings, which also heighten the feelings of safety, comfort, and love. Newborns need hugs because of the biological need of love. Without hugs and the sense of love, an infant will die.[20] To break down barriers to the healing for those who are emotionally shut down from past trauma, you must help them experience the comfort, love, and safety that they longed to receive. That is why the gentle touch, hug, and affirming words of a parent can quickly make a child with a skinned knee feel better.

USING THE LOVE HUG (AND LOVE PAT)

The Love Hug can be used by having the afflicted person simply cross their arms over their chest, resting their hands on their arm/bicep as they picture Jesus (or any other safe and trusted person) giving them a hug. At the same time, the afflicted person can receive a "love pat" by gently patting one hand then the other on their own arm/bicep as they picture Jesus giving gentle pats of reassurance (or the prayer minister can place a hand on each shoulder and gently give a love pat).

---

20. Thomas Verny MD and John Kelly, *The Secret Life of the Unborn Child* (New York: Dell Publishing, 1981), 152.

Illustration of an afflicted person using the Love Hug.

Use one or more of the following Love Hug methods that best corresponds to what you need to accomplish: 1) releasing trauma; 2) receiving comfort; 3) restoring the mind-body connection.

1. RELEASING TRAUMA LOVE HUG

Purpose: To be used when people feel stuck, numb, blank, confused, cannot identify emotions/memories/thoughts, cannot feel love from others or from God, and have generally negative thoughts and feelings.

Explanation: Your mind has been created to take in information during waking hours and sort out that information during sleeping hours. The mind will automatically process the information by sorting out what is good and releasing what is not good. One way in which you have been created to release unhealthy things from your mind is through the process of dreaming. Amazingly, if you do not release the traumatic emotion and memory on your own, your brain will automatically try to release it for you during the process of dreaming. One of the major purposes of dreaming is to modulate, lessen, disturbances in emotion and regulate those that are troublesome.[21] This is why you can experience nightmares or traumatic dreams as a way for your mind to release unwanted trauma.

---

21. "The Science of Sleep: Regulating Emotions and the Twenty-Four Hour Mind," *Farnam Street*, https://fs.blog/2017/03/twenty-four-hour-mind-rosalind-cartwright/ (accessed June 25, 2018).

Dreams mainly occur in the rapid-eye movement (REM) stage of sleep, when brain activity is high and resembles that of being awake. Your eyes move rapidly back and forth to integrate the right and left sides of your brain, in order to sort and release the things that brought concerns during the day. The right side of the brain processes emotion and the left side processes memory. Both sides of the brain are important to process information, make a balanced decision, and retain or release emotion and memory from daily experiences.

God created the REM process during dreaming to prevent unhealthiness by ensuring that your mind releases and is cleansed of unwanted emotions and memory. However, the cleansing does not fully work unless you are able to talk out your dreams by describing the details and identifying and releasing the feelings associated with them. For example, repeated negative dreams or nightmares can be evidence that you are feeling unsafe and/or your mind has been unsuccessful in releasing unwanted emotion and memory.

The good news is that you can use the Love Hug to establish a sense of protection and love for the afflicted person to feel safe enough to release blocked emotion and memory the way God intended. In addition, when you use the "love pat" by gently patting one hand then the other on your arm/bicep, you are simply using the same bilateral movements God created to function within your mind in order to release unwanted or blocked emotion and memory during the natural healing process. You can use the Love Hug and love pat at any time as you pray or talk in ministry to promote a deeper and faster permanent release of emotions and memories. The results can vary depending on the person's willingness to "feel" better, and their receptivity to trusting/receiving help or love from others.

Love Hug Instructions: Use the Love Hug (and love pat) technique simultaneously with any of the other steps or prayers found in this chapter.

The prayer minister can demonstrate the technique for the afflicted person while saying,

1. "You can do the Love Hug by crossing your arms over your chest, resting your hands on your arm or bicep, as you think of Jesus [or another safe person] giving you a hug." (See Love Hug illustration above.)

2. "Continue with the love pat by gently patting one hand then the other on your arm or bicep as you think of Jesus [or another safe person] giving you a 'love pat,' letting you know how much you are loved. You will alternate each hand patting your arm, i.e., right, left, right, left. Gently pat at double the speed of your relaxed heart rate." (Or the prayer minister can place a hand on each shoulder and gently give a love pat.)

Option to say: "This love pat naturally promotes the same biological functions created by God to help your mind sort through and release unwanted or blocked emotion and memory. It will encourage a sense of release, calm, and healing in your mind and body."

Suggestions:

+ As the afflicted person gently pats, the prayer minister can give encouraging words, such as, "See yourself handing the emotion over to Jesus [or another safe person]," "This is old emotion; it's safe now to release it," "It was never God's plan for you to go through this or feel this way."

+ If the afflicted person is afraid, insecure, or in need of more comfort, they can imagine themselves standing in a protected bubble with Jesus or the safe person during the Love Hug process.

+ If the afflicted person's feelings become more intense, keep reassuring them as they release their hurts through talking, tears, sobbing, yells, or whatever it takes to release the emotion. If they experience more emotion than they can handle, they can stop patting and, with their eyes open or closed, picture Jesus (or another safe person) comforting them. Encourage the person with a comfort prayer, and reassure them that it is normal to release a large amount of pain through this process. If needed, invite them to seek out a prayer minister or counseling professional experienced in releasing emotional trauma.

2. COMFORT AND REVELATION LOVE HUG

Purpose: To be used for increasing a sense of peace and calmness to the mind and body; increasing a sense of confidence and feelings of love from God; hearing and/or sensing a deeper connection with the Holy Spirit; receiving more guidance, direction, reassurance, godly revelation, insight, and love; or improving the healing journey and relationship with God.

Explanation: There are many people who rarely receive a comforting hug, pat on the back, or words of affirmation. As part of the restoration process, ask the afflicted person to perform the Love Hug as they picture Jesus (or another safe person) hugging them, as the prayer minister speaks comforting words of reassurance. When you use the "love pat" by gently patting one hand and then the other on your arm/bicep at a slower rate, the sensory nerve endings are stimulated, which heightens hearing as well as feelings of reassurance, comfort, and love that may be needed during restoration of the heart and mind. The Comfort and Revelation Love Hug, along with the love pat, can increase a sense of love from their heavenly Father that perhaps was never felt before. It is an amazing step for affirmation and encouragement. The results can very depending on the person's willingness to "feel" better, and their receptivity to trusting/receiving help or love from others.

Instructions: Use the Love Hug and love pat after releasing trauma to promote the aforementioned purposes.

The prayer minister can demonstrate the technique for the afflicted person while saying:

1. "You can do the Love Hug by crossing your arms over your chest, resting your hands on your arm or bicep, as you think of Jesus [or another safe person] giving you a hug." (See Love Hug illustration on p. 90.)

2. "Continue with the love pat by gently patting one hand then the other on your arm or bicep as you think of Jesus [or another safe person] giving a 'love pat,' letting you know how much you are loved. You will alternate each hand patting your arm, i.e., right, left, right, left. Gently pat at the speed of your relaxed heart rate." (Or the prayer minister can place a hand on each shoulder and gently give a love pat.)

Option to say: "This love pat naturally promotes the same biological functions created by God to help your mind receive a sense of pease, confidence, love, revelation, direction, and reassurance."

Suggestions:

+ As the afflicted person gently pats, the prayer minister can place a hand on their shoulder while providing encouraging words, such as, "Jesus is with you," "You are safe now," "You are loved."

+ Use this step while you pray, talk, think of positive memories, or when giving a father- or mother-blessing prayer. These are listed under "Additional Prayers" in this chapter.

+ Whenever needed (or after a memory is cleared), you have the option for the person to use this Love Hug and ask the Holy Spirit for more guidance, godly revelation and insight, love, or whatever they need for the healing journey and improving their relationship with God.

3. RESTORING THE MIND-BODY CONNECTION LOVE HUG

Purpose: To be used when the afflicted person feels disconnection between the mind and body or feels disconnected and cannot hear from God. Can also be used to promote mind-body integration toward the healing of conditions related to disassociation symptoms (separating emotions resulting from trauma from the physical body), head trauma, and other conditions associated with mental/emotional shutdown and mind/body/spirit disconnection.

Explanation: The mind will automatically separate itself, or shut down, as a result of acute emotional or physical trauma as a way to protect itself from the trauma (this includes head/brain injuries). Mind-body responses may also include disassociation of the mind and body as a result of medical or emotional issues. The love pat movements, with the gentle bilateral movements of one hand and then the other on the arm/bicep, can assist in integrating both sides of the brain to potentially reintroduce a connection of the mind and body. As I mentioned earlier, the physical touch and gentle patting increases the sensory nerve endings and heightens your thinking and feeling. This process has been successful in helping unemotional people begin to identify feelings, decrease disassociative symptoms, and spur mind-body integration and coordination. The results can vary depending on the person's willingness to "feel" better, and their receptivity to trusting/receiving help from others.

Instructions: Use the Love Hug (and love pat) during and after the prayers below and/or healing ministry to promote the aforementioned purposes.

The prayer minister can demonstrate the technique for the afflicted person while saying:

1. "You can do the Love Hug by crossing your arms over your chest, resting your hands on your arm or bicep, as you think of Jesus [or another safe person] giving you a hug." (See Love Hug illustration on p. 90.)

2. "Continue with the love pat by gently patting one hand then the other on your arm or bicep as you think of Jesus [or another safe person] giving a 'love pat,' letting you

know how much you are loved. You will alternate each hand patting your arm, ie, right, left, right, left. Gently pat at the speed of your relaxed heart rate." (Or the prayer minister can place a hand on each shoulder and gently give a love pat.)

Option to say: "This love pat naturally promotes the same biological functions created by God to help the potential integration of both sides of the brain for mind-body connection, integration, and healing."

Suggestions:

+ Use the Mind-Body Connection Love Hug (and love pat) as you sit quietly, using the prayers below. Ask the Holy Spirit for more revelation, healing, integration, or whatever else you need for your mind-body healing.

RESTORING THE MIND-BODY CONNECTION PRAYERS:

This prayer and can be modified to accommodate the condition or circumstance. Ask the afflicted person to repeat this prayer:

In the name of Jesus, I curse the condition of _____ that has harmed my mind. I forgive myself for my part in the injury, and I forgive any other persons responsible for my injury. I repent for receiving and accepting any part of this condition or diagnosis. I curse any emotional, physical, or cellular memory trauma, as well as all symptoms and complications associated with this injury.

The prayer minister can pray:

In the name of Jesus, I curse the disconnect between [afflicted person's name] mind and body, and any emotional, mental, medical, or physical dysfunction that is causing this disunion. In the name of Jesus, I command the electrical, chemical, magnetic, hormonal, and neurological frequencies in every cell in the mind and body to become in harmony and in balance. In Jesus's name, I command the mind and body of [afflicted person's name] to become healed, become integrated, and be united to function as God intended. In Jesus's name, I declare [afflicted person's name] to receive God's spirit of life, light, love, and peace. I pray for the blood of Jesus to bring healing and wholeness to their mind and body. Thank you, Jesus, for healing.

STEP VI: ADDITIONAL PRAYERS

ADD/ADHD, BIPOLAR, DYSLEXIA AND OTHER CONDITIONS ORIGINATING BEFORE BIRTH

Unhealthy mind-body conditions can begin during the development stages in utero, when the chemical, emotional, hormonal, and environment factors affect the fetus. (See chapter 15 to find specific conditions and emotions.) In addition, if an image of the womb, or a revelation about a condition originating in the womb, comes to your attention during healing prayer, the following prayer may be helpful. This prayer can be used to restore the mind and body, and it can be modified to accommodate the condition or circumstance.

Instructions:

1. Ask the afflicted person to close their eyes and, on a scale of 0–10, rate how much their mind feels as if it is sad, frantic, racing, overwhelmed, or unbalanced. (Zero being complete health, 10 being extreme affliction.)

2. Ask the person to place their hands on their stomach.

3. Ask them to picture themselves in the womb, with Jesus placing His hands on them. The prayer minister can place a hand on the person's head and lower back. (Always ask permission before initiating contact.)

4.   Ask the afflicted person to repeat after you:

In the name of Jesus, I curse the condition of [_____] that was passed down to me through my mother's womb from the previous generations. I forgive my mother, father, and the generations before them for passing on the condition of [_____]. I renounce this condition and do not give it permission or authority to be a part of my life anymore. I repent for receiving and accepting any part of this condition or the diagnosis given to me. In Jesus's name, I curse any symptoms or complications associated with this diagnosis. I accept Jesus in my heart and I receive Your Spirit of life, love, peace, wholeness, and restoration of my mind and body. Thank You, Jesus, for my healing.

This simpler prayer may be repeated by a child, or at any time by an adult:

I forgive you, Mother and Father, for any condition you transferred to me that is not of God. I do not accept this condition in my mind or body. Thank You, God, for restoring my health, as it is in heaven.

5.   Next, the prayer minister can pray this prayer over the afflicted person:

In Jesus's name, I renounce the condition of [_____] and give it no more authority. In Jesus's name, I curse any utero trauma and command the electrical, chemical, magnetic, hormonal, and neurological frequencies in every cell of the mind and body to come into alignment and balance, with proper integration and polarity, as it is in heaven. In Jesus's name, I declare peace and healthy functioning over the mind and body. Thank You, Jesus, for Your healing.

6. Ask the afflicted person to close their eyes and, on a scale of 0–10, rate how much their mind feels as if it is sad, frantic, racing, overwhelmed, or unbalanced. (Zero being complete health, 10 being extreme affliction.) As the number decreases, repeat numbers 1–6 above until the mind feels at zero, or as close as possible.

Review the condition information found in chapter 15, releasing the unwanted emotional connection and pray for restored functioning. For example, for the condition of ADD/ADHD, the afflicted person can forgive their mother for making them anxious in utero (or forgive their mother and father for anxiety created during childhood). They can pray for a peaceful mind and for restoration for their adrenal gland to normal functioning, on earth as it is in heaven.

If the number does not decrease or the mind has minimal improvement:

If the mind condition does not change after a few prayer attempts, this is an indication that the condition originated from past or present-day abusive, chaotic, or overwhelming situations with unresolved traumatic emotions (for example, fear, grief, hurt, sadness, burdens, abuse, etc.).

Releasing symptoms from trauma:

+ Ask the afflicted person for more information about any trauma, hurt, worry, or extreme burdens they had or currently are experiencing. Pray, using **Step II: Prayers for Releasing Trauma.**

+ After the healing prayer, ask the afflicted person to close their eyes and rate, on a scale of 0–10, how much their mind feels as though it is sad, frantic, racing, overwhelmed, and unbalanced. As the number decreases, repeat the aforementioned numbers 1–6 until they rate their mind at zero, or as close as possible.

CANCER OR OTHER DISEASES

The afflicted person can read or repeat after the prayer minister.

> In the name of Jesus, I curse the diagnosis spoken over me and cast out the seed, spirit, and root of (condition's name), and I curse any generational spirits or roots that have carried this condition. I repent for accepting this diagnosis and forgive the healthcare professionals for giving the diagnosis.
>
> I forgive my parents and the generations before them for any involvement with this condition. In Jesus's name, I curse the spirit of death, fear, rejection, abandonment, or any other emotional and physical trauma from the past and present that has contributed to this condition.
>
> In Jesus's name, I command healing to all organs, bone, and tissues affected by this condition to be restored to their healthy function, and I command the electrical, chemical, magnetic, hormonal, and neurological frequencies in every cell, both in the mind and body, to become in harmony and in balance. In Jesus's name, I curse the unhealthy prion cells in the body and declare healthy cells to be restored to normal functioning in all affected areas. In Jesus's name, I declare over my body and mind the spirit of life, love, acceptance, peace, the light of God, and the full restoration of my mind and body to function normally, as I live in the belief that I am healed. Thank You, Jesus, for my healing.

HEAVENLY FATHER'S BLESSING

The prayer minister can place a hand on the afflicted person's head and say this blessing prayer. This prayer can be modified to accommodate the condition or circumstance.

Your heavenly Father wants to say to you, "I see you and I am very proud of you. I think very highly of you, and I will always believe in you. I will always love you, no matter what you have done, because that is how I really feel about you. I do not condemn you. I want to give My favor over your life and give back to you what you have lost. I declare great blessings over you, and I look forward to you growing and succeeding in life. I want you to trust Me and to look to Me for the guidance and the love I would like to give you. I love you. I am your heavenly Daddy."

SPIRITUAL WARFARE PRAYER

The prayer minister can pray this prayer if anyone sees, feels, or senses a sudden darkness, unusual fear, the movement of objects, shadows, or odd and intense behaviors with the afflicted person.

By the authority I have in Jesus, I command this spirit of [darkness, oppression, etc.] to be bound and sent away. I plead the blood of Jesus over [afflicted person's name] and, in the name of Jesus, I declare peace into their mind and body. Thank You, Jesus, for Your protection.

RELEASING GENERATIONAL CONDITIONS AND CURSES

This includes parents and extended family with medical conditions, mental illness, suicide, or involvement in the occult and other demonic activity. The prayer minister can pray, or the afflicted person can repeat the prayer.

In the name of Jesus, I declare the blood of Jesus to come between me and the generations before me as a wall of separation. I cancel every assignment of darkness and remove every right of [name the condition] to afflict me. I renounce and give no more authority for this generational issue or cause to be in my life. I forgive the generations before me and receive the blood of Jesus to cleanse my mind and body and call to me my righteous inheritance and blessings of that generation. Thank You, Jesus, for my freedom.

The Addendum lists the Steps for Healing Prayer, Love Hug Steps, and additional prayers without the detailed explanations, to be easily photocopied or displayed on your e-reader as you pray and minister anywhere you go.

11

PRACTICAL TIPS FOR BREAKING THROUGH TO HEALING

WHAT TO DO WHEN SOMEONE CANNOT REMEMBER PAST MEMORIES

There will be times when you ask the afflicted person to think of a past memory or emotion and they will not be able to remember part or all of their past. As I mentioned before, when someone experiences excessively unhealthy emotions (trauma), the mind may not properly process all the information, so the emotion, images, sounds, and physical sensations become stuck in a traumatic state and the mind suppresses the information in order to protect the mind and body from shock. As a result, the suppressed state of mind becomes a barrier to healing.

I believe that God has the ability to break through that shock and heal the trauma. However, it is also true that God created you with emotions and a free will to choose what to do with your emotions. If you are not ready or unwilling to release the emotion, God will not force it. He also will not condemn or manipulate your decision to hold on to the emotions or memories. To move into healing, the following simple steps will help the afflicted person begin to connect with the past:

+ Have the afflicted person picture him- or herself as a child or teen, as if they are watching a home movie of the situation in which they were raised.

+ Ask them to guess what they would see, feel, and think as they picture themselves living in that situation. How did other people or family members act toward them? I recommend the afflicted person use the Step V: Love Hug technique in chapter 10 to identify deeper emotion and memory.

+ When the unhealthy thoughts and feelings are identified by the afflicted person, simultaneously using Step II with Step IV in chapter 10 will bring release and restoration.

For example, if the afflicted person only remembers that their father left the family and their mother struggled to make ends meet, but they do not remember many other images or feelings, have them picture themself as a child in their home, the way they just described it to you. Have them *guess* what they think the events and feelings would have been like for a child in that home during that time. Keep asking more questions about what they would *guess* the situation and feelings would have been like. The afflicted person would benefit from using Step V: Releasing Trauma— Love Hug to increase the release of thoughts and feelings.

KNOWN AND UNKNOWN TRAUMA

When you ask the afflicted person when or why the problem or condition started, they will give one of two types of responses, which were described in chapter 4: known trauma or unknown trauma.

Known Trauma

This is when an event or person that caused the condition can be identified. This may include the details of injuries, actions, and words that were tangibly experienced during the hurtful time. This may also include emotional, physical, sexual, and verbal abuse or other forms of domestic violence. These emotions and memories will usually surface when you ask the Holy Spirit to bring them to mind.

Unknown Trauma

This is when the afflicted person cannot identify why or who caused the condition, or when there is no known reason for the condition. These memories are usually suppressed and the person will require more assistance to help retrieve them. As is often the case, the more trauma experienced, the deeper the suppression of the emotion and memory will be. In addition, if the trauma is from early childhood, children typically do not know how to assign words to their emotions, or they are not able to express emotions because of fear or lack of encouragement by caregivers. As a result, there may not always be emotions associated with the memory. Consequently, you will need to ask the person to guess what a child would feel in that situation.

For both known and unknown trauma, it would be helpful for the afflicted person to use Step V: Releasing Trauma—Love Hug while sharing information, in order to break through the deeper trauma.

WHAT TO DO WHEN SOMEONE CANNOT IDENTIFY OR EXPRESS FEELINGS

As a child, your expression of feelings should be a natural reaction to your experiences. How your caregivers responded to those expressions created an imprint regarding how you will express yourself for the rest of your life—unless you are taught differently. For example, if your parents become angry or you are told to "stop your crying!" when emotions are expressed, you will learn to believe that feelings are not safe to release. Consequently, if you do not express your feelings, you will have difficulty releasing trauma and will subsequently create a barrier to the healing process.

I knew a man who experienced much frustration and anger at work, but rarely expressed his thoughts because he was afraid something "bad" would happen. At home, whenever his wife became upset with him, he would either keep quiet or walk away. This would upset the wife even more and result in further problems. The man commented to me that he was frequently irritable, tense, and anxious. He also experienced headaches and had difficulty concentrating. This became a normal way of life for him. He grew up in a family in which feelings and emotions were seldom expressed or talked about. And whenever he did express his feelings, he was sent to his room. When he received ministry and understood that God created us to express our feelings, he felt freer to identify past feelings.

A woman told me how she would socially withdraw and emotionally shut down whenever she was in an argument with others. After prolonged conflict, she experienced unexplained periods of irritability, anxiety, crying spells, sleeping problems, and depression. As a child, she often found herself standing between her parents during their arguments. She recalled this experience as being an upsetting and anxious moment. As a child, she always kept her feelings inside, fearing that expressing them would make her parents angrier, and add to their reasons for leaving. As an adult, the woman continued to shut down emotionally and was not able find the right words to describe her feelings.

What these people, and so many others, have in common is that they were not expressing what they felt because of what they believed from hurtful events in the past. The good news is that God is greater than whatever the afflicted person faces, and you have the power to help them find freedom. In his book *Peace, Love and Healing*, physician and author Bernie S. Siegel explores the significance of releasing all feelings. He writes, "It's important to express all your feelings, including the unpleasant ones, because once they're out, they lose their power over you; they can't tie you up in knots anymore. Letting them out is a call for help and a 'live' message to your body."[22]

---

22. Bernie S. Siegel MD, *Peace, Love and Healing* (New York: Harper & Row, 1989), 29.

HELPING OTHERS TO EXPRESS FEELINGS

God never intended people to be consumed with inner turmoil and remain silent about it. The following are suggestions to help a person to express their feelings:

1. Make the person feel safe by using the *active listening* techniques found in chapter 5.

2. Ask the afflicted person to guess how they would feel and what they would think as they picture themselves living with their condition or circumstances. Give the person several feeling words to consider since this may be the first time they have talked about their feelings. Through this process, have the afflicted person use the Step V: Love Hug technique in chapter 10 to promote deeper exploration and release of emotion and memory.

3. Tell the person that expressing emotions is how God originally created us, as natural as having tears to express joy or sadness.

4. Have the person pray for the Holy Spirit to bring guidance and revelation in identifying their feelings.

5. As the person begins to express their feelings, give them words of encouragement.

You are born with emotions as a natural function, to release energy and communicate with others. If you do not use these sources of expression in daily life, you will not experience the joy of life to its fullest potential.

WHAT TO DO WHEN SOMEONE IS NOT READY TO FORGIVE

Unforgiveness is one of the most common hindrances to healing of the heart, mind, and body. The act of forgiveness is a personal choice, a spiritual action, and an essential step to obtain healing and restoration. However, if forgiveness is so important, it does not make sense why the afflicted person would hold on to unforgiveness. But if they are still consumed with some inner struggle (anger, hurt, or injustice), the emotion will blind them from seeing how illogical or unhealthy it is to hold on to unforgiveness. Forgiveness is about making a logical choice to release someone or something from an event that caused injustice or harm. Since every hurtful event causes an emotional trauma, the person must reveal and release the unhealthy emotion before they feel justified or safe to forgive others. If you observe the afflicted person doing any of the following, it is a good sign they are not ready to forgive during healing prayer process:

+ difficulty talking about feelings

+ not wanting to let go of past unhealthy emotion

+ wanting to remain angry or get even

+ afraid of being hurt again or afraid to be vulnerable

If a person does not want to forgive, they typically believe there is a strong reason to hold on to the emotion. In these cases, common Christian phrases like "just give it to Jesus" or "take it to the cross" will not be enough for them to fully let go and forgive. Consequently, the prayer minister needs a stronger reason to persuade the person to release the unhealthy emotion and move toward forgiveness. The prayer minister can try the following exercise to help the afflicted person to forgive:

> [The prayer minister is to make a fist with their left hand and an open palm with their right hand. Then say to the afflicted person:]

> When you were hurt or an injustice happened, another person [or event] overpowered you in a way that created emotion in you. This fist represents the person (or event) that hurt you. This open hand is you experiencing the emotion. Since this open hand is you when you were hurt, you attached yourself to the person [or event] causing you pain.

[Place your open right hand over the fist of your left hand. Next, say to the afflicted person:]

As long as your feelings remain attached to this person [or event], you are giving them [or it] power over you. You are in emotional and spiritual bondage to that person [or event]. You were wronged by this person, and you are still the one carrying around the hurt. Do you want that anymore? Do you want that person [or event] to have that much power over you? Do you want to remain powerless? Are you ready to feel better?

[As you separate the right and left hands, showing your fist on the left and your open palm on the right, you can say to the afflicted person:]

All I want to do now is separate you from the wrongdoer. You don't need to like what happened. You don't have to forgive them yet. Just picture yourself with your emotions separate from what happened so you do not need to be controlled by that person [or event].

[Now the prayer minister should use the Step V: Releasing Trauma—Love Hug technique simultaneously with Step II: Prayers for Releasing Trauma in chapter 10.]

WHAT TO DO WHEN SOMEONE CANNOT RELEASE ANGER, HURT, OR RESENTMENT

When the afflicted person cannot release anger, hurt, or resentment, this is confirmation there are hurts in the past, or that they are currently living in an unsafe situation. You may hear phrases such as "I don't want them in my life," "I can't stop being angry at them," "I hate them; I can't believe they did this," "How could they," "It's not fair," "I can't do anything about it," or "I can't forgive them." Unreleased, suppressed emotion will consume them and create a barrier to realizing how unhealthy it is to hold on to the hurt and injustice. The afflicted person may be holding on to the emotion for reasons such as:

+ Protection from being hurt again
+ Fear of appearing weak or vulnerable
+ Not receiving justice or compensation for the wrongdoing
+ Continuing to suffer in the current offense because a similar past offense was never released

The following steps will break down barriers to begin healing:

1. Ask or tell the afflicted person any of the following:

+ Do you like feeling this way or does this feeling help your situation?
+ Do you have hurt or resentment from situations that are continuing to happen?
+ Do you still have hurt or resentment from past situations?
+ As long as you hold on to these feelings, you give the people and situations power over you. Are you ready to change how you feel?

2. Begin the Steps for Healing Prayer (see chapter 10)

3. If the prayee continues to have difficulty releasing emotions of hurt, anger, or resentment:

+ Ask if there is earlier childhood trauma that may need to be resolved. Pray for the Holy Spirit to find the earlier trauma and continue to follow the Steps for Healing Prayer.
+ The afflicted person is holding on to these feelings because they are currently in a situation that is hurtful, unsafe, or a burden.

Use Step V in chapter 10 to reveal and release any earlier memory or emotion, and/or suggest time away or complete separation from the hurtful person if there is a threat of physical or emotional harm.

+ Forgive self and family for any generational line of abuse, neglect, etc. (See Prayers for Generational Conditions and Curses in chapter 10.)

+ If intense emotion persists, pray for Jesus to protect the person and recommend that they seek additional Christian counseling from a trained professional.

WHAT TO DO WHEN JESUS IS NOT WANTED IN THE HEALING PROCESS

What if the person does not want to involve Jesus in the healing process? What if they are angry at God, or Jesus, and want nothing to do with Him?

For some, forcing Jesus into the healing process can cause more harm. It is important that you have an alternative way to create a safe environment so the afflicted person will feel it is safe to reveal deeper issues and receive healing.

First, you need to understand that when someone does not want the help of Jesus, it is most often because the person does not feel safe after feeling abused, rejected, abandoned, or unprotected by authority figures (or by Jesus) during an early-life traumatic event. Another strong reason is when prayers are not answered during traumatic events, which can create disappointment, hurt, confusion, abandonment, distrust, and feelings of not being loved. When these events happen, especially in childhood, the young mind cannot make sense out of the trauma. As a result, the mind creates unhealthy beliefs and thoughts, such as *I cannot trust or rely on God for help, I am not protected by God, I am alone,* or *I'm not good enough to be loved or go to heaven.* The most common belief is that of feeling unprotected or unloved. When these mind imprints are not released, it creates a crisis of faith and a struggle to believe in healing throughout life. Before you utilize Jesus as a method for healing, it is important to ask if you can invite Jesus into the memory, since the afflicted person may not reveal their distrust of God, and may not want to disappoint the praying minister.

Some indications that the afflicted person may not want Jesus involved:

1. The person expresses negative comments or feelings about God or Jesus when describing the trauma events.

2. The person has had never had a relationship with Jesus, or they are of a different cultural or spiritual belief that does not recognize Jesus as Healer or the Son of God.

3. When Jesus is introduced into the healing process, the person:

    a. does not respond positively or their prayers show little progress and limited effectiveness.

    b. becomes more agitated, emotionally distant, or shut down.

HELPING THE AFFLICTED PERSON TO FEEL SAFE

When the afflicted person feels unsafe to release unhealthy emotions (especially when thinking of Jesus), memories, or beliefs, healing of traumatic memories will become more difficult. Feeling unsafe may be evident when the person:

+ has difficulty talking about their thoughts or feelings regarding a memory.

+ does not remember or want to "go to the memory" in their mind.

+ has difficulty trusting others and Jesus, specifically regarding a memory.

It is important to transition the afflicted person toward a feeling of safety before the process of identifying and releasing occurs.

The following steps can be incorporated when using Step II in chapter 10:

1. Ask the afflicted person if they can imagine someone whom they trust (a friend, family member, or themselves as an adult) who can stand in as their protector. As they picture the trusted person protecting them, you can continue the healing process two ways:

   a. Ask the person if you can continue the healing process by praying to the God.

   b. Or, ask the person if you can continue the healing process by using the term "Spirit of truth" rather than God.

   c. If the afflicted person does not want any spirituality in the healing process, continue only using the designated trusted person.

2. If the person cannot think of anyone to protect them, ask if you (as a prayer minister) can be seen as the protector. Although I do not recommend the prayer minister image to be continually used as a protector, your goal is to release enough pain to eventually introduce the afflicted person to Jesus.

3. Ask the person to picture themselves in a protective bubble with the safe person (this can also be used with Jesus when appropriate) with the hurtful person (or event) outside the bubble. This is a simple and powerful image to create a feeling of safety.

I was praying for a woman named Cherie who remembered a childhood memory when she was sexually traumatized by her grandfather. When I used the Steps for Healing Prayer, she was direct about her anger at God and did not want Jesus with her in the memory. She said, "Jesus didn't protect me, so I don't want Him there." I honored that request and asked if she had a favorite family member whom she felt safe to be with. She mentioned her uncle, so I had her picture herself inside a large protective bubble with her uncle and grandfather standing on the outside. When she felt safe from the grandfather, she was able to release the emotional trauma. I then asked if she would allow Jesus to appear in the image. She agreed and I asked what Jesus was doing in her mental picture. She pictured Jesus holding her, and saying everything was going to be all right. As I asked her to fold her arms across her chest as she pictured Jesus holding her, I put my hand on her head and prayed the Father's blessing over her. Cherie began to release her tears of relief and grateful joy, because she was finally free.

HELPING THE AFFLICTED PERSON TO TRUST JESUS

When emotional trauma causes a person to not trust the presence of Jesus, the more love and compassion of Jesus you show, the more progress you will make. In order to help the afflicted person to trust Jesus, it is important to reveal and release as much traumatic emotion and ungodly beliefs as possible. The emotion will block the person's ability to see, feel, and trust the truth. This is especially true if they were abused, neglected, or abandoned by a parent, especially a father. Your experiences with your earthly father will often affect your beliefs and expectations for your heavenly Father. As a result, this ungodly belief needs to change. To do this, use the following options:

1. Show compassion by validating what the person has been through and the pain it has caused. For more details, review the Active Listening section in the chapter 5.

2. To identify and release deeper emotions and memories, simultaneously use Step II and Step V in chapter 10. Because of their lack of trust, replace the image of Jesus with another safe person, as mentioned above.

3. One major reason for not trusting God is due to the lack of a loving relationship with God. Have them consider the

children in their life, either theirs or the children of family members or friends. Then ask the following questions (alter them as needed):

a. Do you love children (or your children), no matter what they do?

b. If a child did something wrong, would you still love them?

c. Is God your heavenly Father? Are you a child of God?

d. If you can love your child, no matter what they have done, why can't God, as your heavenly Parent, love you, no matter what you or someone else has done?

Here are additional questions for them to ponder if they continue to struggle with trusting God/Jesus:

1. Why is your love for your child greater than God's love for you as His child?

2. What makes your love for a child more important than God's love for you as His child?

3. If you would protect a child, why do you think that God would not love and protect you?

4. Can you now allow God to love you, just as you love the children in your life?

After you go through these questions, have the person close their eyes and picture Jesus with them. Ask them what they see Jesus doing. If ungodly beliefs or emotions persist, that is usually an indication of the existence of emotional pain from some other important person in their life that needs to be revealed and released. Repeat Step II in the Steps for Healing Prayer.

WHAT TO DO WHEN HEALING COMES IN LAYERS

Even though Jesus is able to bring healing through a single simple prayer, there may be times when healing does not come until you work through many issues or "layers." This type of healing can take place over a few hours or it may require many prayer sessions to release multiple harmful issues. I have also seen situations in which prayers only bring temporary improvement, or in which the symptoms return within a few days or weeks. This can be evidence you need to expand your search to reveal the multiple layers of issues, such as unconfessed sin, unforgiveness, or emotional trauma. (See chapter 12, Expanding Your Search When Healing Doesn't Occur.) Think of it as peeling an onion. You may need many prayers to identify and release layer after layer of damage caused by important people in your life who disappointed or harmed you over the years. There may be times when God can wipe away all the layers in one prayer, while other times, He will allow you to reveal and identify each incident, one after another, until you get to the core of your onion. For the afflicted person, the intensity of the emotion, the significance of the incidents, and the level of vulnerability inflicted by the injustice (i.e., fear of something bad happening), all play a part in how effectively the person will be able to release emotion and memory.

God is powerful enough to wipe away every negative and harmful emotion, but He also respects the freedom of choice He gave you, in case you choose to hold on to what you are not ready to release. This is where the prayer minister can create a safe environment for the afflicted person to release either each hurtful incident (layer) or go directly to the original core issues. Once the original core trauma is released, the subsequent layers of childhood traumas will often automatically begin to break off.

It is important to listen, watch for clues, and be attuned to what the Holy Spirit wants you to do as you pray. Having to pray repeatedly over an illness is not necessarily a sign of a lack of faith or a weak prayer life, but it may be a sign there may be more issues to be identified and released. Some of the reasons trauma comes in layers may be due to the following:

1. Separate traumatic events over a period of time. This may include disappointment, loss, and injustices caused by family, friends, work situations, etc. Each event should be revealed, released, and restored using the Steps for Healing Prayer, unless you are led to pray over all the issues in one bundle.

2. Multiple traumatic experiences from the same life event. If your senses become bombarded with emotion from the effects of trauma, such as repeated abuse (i.e., repeated molestation by the same person) or an auto accident with many traumatic experiences (i.e., feeling trapped in the car, painful ride to the hospital, seeing someone die, etc.), you may need healing in layers. You will need to pray for the initial trauma as well as each layer of new trauma, which may include things that occurred before the trauma, during the trauma, and living with the lasting effects of the trauma. All of these layers should be revealed, released, and restored using the Steps for Healing Prayer, unless you are led to pray over all the issues in one bundle.

3. The longer the afflicted person has been living with the condition, the more likely they have created a life or identity around the condition. You will need to pray for the initial onset of the trauma, the discomfort of living with the effects of the trauma, the fear and disappointment of not being healed, and the transforming of their mind from living as a sick person to living as a healthy person. (See Romans 12:1–2.) The person may resist the release of long-term emotion out of fear that they will not receive their healing, and out of fear of how they will live differently after they are healed. All of these layers should be revealed, released, and restored using the Steps for Healing Prayer.

I once prayed for a woman who hit her head on a wet floor after a slip and fall at work. She suffered a concussion and was unable to work for months due to migraines and chronic pain in her neck, shoulders, and back. Eventually, she had to take a forced leave from her job because the pain did not allow her to return to work. When I first prayed for the initial trauma at her workplace, she was able to walk away pain free. When I saw her a week later, however, her pain had returned. When I asked her for more information, she gave me details about her injury I had not previously been aware of. It seems that after her fall and head injury, she had laid on the floor in agony, terrified that she would never walk again. I realized that the powerful emotion of lying helpless on the floor had not been previously dealt with. When I asked her to picture Jesus with her on that floor, she was able to release the fear and her pain was gone. When I saw her a few weeks later, the pain had returned again. At that time, I realized I had not asked about her time after the accident, when she was recuperating at home, feeling helpless and hopeless. It seemed that she was experiencing more intense levels of feelings of helplessness than expected from the accident. We asked God if there was some experience in her childhood that created extreme helplessness. When God was able to reveal and release a childhood event of helplessness, the pain left her body again. Each time we met, God revealed more and more layers of hurt from her accident, including anger at her employer, grief at her loss of physical independence, and feelings of depression from living with the injury.

The point is, when healing does not happen or the condition returns, always expand your search for more details surrounding the events. As I said before, with every physical trauma, there is always a corresponding emotion (whether you feel it or not). In almost every case, emotional trauma will follow the occurance of a physical injury. Even though I do not need to hear all the traumatic details for God to heal (He already knows them), there is still a need to use Step II of the Steps for Healing Prayer to identify the major emotions encountered before, during, and after a traumatc event.

MISUNDERSTOOD DOMESTIC VIOLENCE TRAUMA

Unfortunately, domestic violence and neglect are all too common, and are widely misunderstood causes of trauma. Most people associate the phrase domestic violence only when there is physical abuse. However, domestic violence also incorporates a wide spectrum of unhealthy treatment that often becomes an underlying issue that needs to be identified and released. I strongly recommend you become familiar with these various forms of domestic violence that cause trauma. Anyone who can relate with one or more of the following indicators is living in a hurtful or neglectful domestic situation.

+ **Emotional abuse:** Criticism, silent treatment, mind games, using the past against you, telling others about your personal matters without your permission.

+ **Verbal abuse:** Name calling, belittling, bullying, judgmental, sarcastic statements, and constant yelling.

+ **Intimidation:** Instilling fear or control by using threats, gestures, menacing looks and body language, throwing things or destroying property, slamming doors, and punching walls.

+ **Sexual abuse:** Forcing you to have sex against your will, treating you like an object, belittling or criticizing you when you do not want sex, unwanted sexual touching or groping, and forcibly revealing your private body parts.

+ **Threats/emotional blackmail:** Verbalizing or carrying out threats to get what they want or making menacing statements and gestures toward you or a family member.

+ **Physical abuse:** Hitting, shoving, slapping, choking, kicking, pulling hair, twisting arms, and excessive spanking or physical discipline.

- **Economic abuse**: Keeping you from obtaining or quitting a job, controlling your money by limiting access to bank accounts, or issuing threats attached to money.

- **Using superior attitude**: Treating you like a servant, not including you in family decisions, acting like the "master of the castle," or lording authority over you.

- **Religious abuse**: Using God or Scripture as a means to control your behavior, cruel judgments, punishments, or criticism, or issuing statements such as, "And you call yourself a Christian," "God will get you for that," "God is not pleased with you," or "You're going to hell."

- **Neglect and unknown trauma**: Forced isolation, denied basic needs for extended periods, not receiving affirmation, encouragement, affection, or nurturing (i.e., not being told you are loved and valued, not provided with physical affection such as hugs and kisses).

OTHER HINDRANCES THAT CAN BLOCK HEALING

If healing does not happen, ask the Holy Spirit to guide you to any of the following hindrances that may be blocking healing. Even if the afflicted person received ministry in the past for many of the following hindrances, it is common that unresolved past emotions will not be addressed (for more details about these hindrances to healing and how to address them, I recommend my book *Finding Victory When Healing Doesn't Happen*):

- **Unforgiveness toward others, God, or self**: Ask the person if there is anyone they need to forgive. I once prayed five times for a woman with a neck injury from an accident with little change. When I asked her about forgiveness (I should have asked earlier), she forgave the other driver for hitting her car, as well as her mother for other reasons. In that moment, her neck problem improved.

+ **Sin:** Ask the person about unresolved sin in their life, or if they believe God is mad at them for past sins. Sin is easy to clear by simply asking God for forgiveness. (See Ephesians 1:7.) Either have the person ask for forgiveness for each sin or ask God to forgive all their sins at one time.

+ **Unbelief, unworthiness:** This can include not believing healing is for you, not believing you are worthy of healing, and not believing you are good enough to be healed. What a person says and how they use their words will be a telltale sign of this (see chapter 12, Expanding Your Search When Healing Doesn't Occur). Ask if they believe they can be healed and if they feel worthy to be healed. If they do not feel worthy, use the Steps for Healing Prayer to work through the unworthiness.

+ **Fear and doubt:** Because of unresolved feelings of rejection, lack of love, loss, disappointment, and emotional or physical traumas, the person will continue to interpret life, healing, salvation, and God from a place of fear and doubt. The person typically doubts the truth about healing, fears healing will not happen for them, or fears their life situations will become worse. Use the Steps for Healing Prayer to work through this.

+ **Spiritual warfare:** This includes generational curses, spells, fears, behaviors, and atmospheric spirits caused when demons spiritually affect the mind and body in ways that would appear to be outside rational thought. Demons cannot completely take over the body and mind of a born again Christian, but they can influence, misguide, oppress, harm, and overwhelm the mind, body, and spirit. As a believer, you have the power and authority over the enemy. (See Mark 16:17.)

12

EXPANDING YOUR SEARCH WHEN HEALING DOESN'T OCCUR

When you have prayed for healing several times and still there is no change, it is time to *expand your search* to reveal earlier emotions or memories that may be barriers to the healing process. When barriers from the past are identified and released, the soul will be free to flow in healing. Even Jesus understood the importance of the past when He asked the father about his possessed son in Mark 9:21: *"How long has this been happening to him?"* To help with your search, ask the Holy Spirit to provide revelation and guidance as you go through these steps. You can use the process of expanding your search during Step II of the Steps for Healing Prayer (see chapter 10), incorporating the following suggestions:

1. GET MORE DETAILS

[Ask the afflicted person,] "Was the condition or emotion caused by an event, an offender, or was there no identifiable reason?" Have the person briefly describe the experience, including the feelings they had when it happened. If they can't identify a reason for the condition, ask them when they first experienced the symptoms, and what stressful events happened to them, or to others close to them, in the months (or year) before the symptoms started. As you get more details do the following:

LISTEN TO WORDS SPOKEN AND PAY ATTENTION TO HOW THEY SAY IT

Words will often give away the origin of the original trauma. As I mentioned before, unresolved emotion from trauma early in life can be so powerful, a person will continue to react in behavior and words appropriate for a person at the age of the original trauma. The person may not be aware of their childlike words or reactions, but you will be.

For example, while ministering with the afflicted person, you may hear phrases such as…

+ "Life is so unfair."
+ "I'm so bad; how can God love someone like me?"
+ "I can't move forward."
+ "I'm afraid of the future."
+ "Nobody loves me."
+ "I'm not a good person."

In addition, you may hear words such as *helpless, hopeless, stuck, limited, restricted, unworthy, undeserving, can't, afraid, unwanted, alone, angry, empty, unloved, inadequate, stupid, dumb,* etc. Although you are hearing adult words, they actually represent childhood emotion releasing in ways the afflicted person could not or did not express as a wounded child. In essence, you are hearing adult words that represent their wounded childhood.

Annette felt a number six pain level in her shoulder for four months but was not aware of the cause. We prayed a few times but the pain only dropped to a level four, so I expanded my search by asking what happened five months ago (one month before the pain started). Annette felt hurt and resentful when her brother made unkind remarks at a family reunion. When I asked if anything happened physically, she remembered doing some exercises and felt a pain in her shoulders, but forgot all about it. I asked what it felt like to live with both her brother's comments and the shoulder pain. Annette said she felt like a victim and helpless to do anything about it. Since I knew her words did not match her adult appearance and capabilities, it was clear these feelings came from earlier in her life. When we asked the Holy Spirit to take Annette to a past memory when she felt like a victim, she recalled a time in her childhood when her brother physically hurt her shoulder. At the time, when she told her mother what happened, her brother denied it and her mother believed him. This was the point when Annette developed a lifelong resentment for her brother, as well as the false belief that she was not good enough. After she released this emotion, she was able to forgive her brother and mother, and her shoulder pain disappeared without further prayer.

Typically, the way you handle situations in the present is affected by how your caretakers treated you, or how you saw them handle similar experiences in the past. If you did not learn a better way of coping, or if you were not allowed to heal wounded emotions, you will continue to think and behave the same way in adulthood. Consequently, how you learned to handle life circumstances associated with pain, suffering, and trauma as a child will reflect in how you behave and respond to life as an adult.

The following are indicators of someone living with wounded emotions from the past:

- neediness
- worry
- fear
- anger
- arguing
- complaining
- whining
- inadequacy

+ victim mentality

+ panic attacks

+ self-criticism

+ defensiveness

+ worries about personal appearance or what people think about you

+ emotional shut down

+ emotional and physical withdrawal

+ verbal or behavior outbursts

+ adult temper tantrums

+ avoiding eye contact

+ fear of conflict

+ slamming doors

+ unworthiness or undeserving of good things

If you see or hear emotional expressions or phrases as listed above, that person has experienced past unresolved traumas that intensify the expression of emotion in present-day circumstances. This creates a hindrance to healing. Before healing can occur, you will have to expand the search so that God can reveal, release, and resolve these trauma experiences from the past.

LOCATION OF THE CONDITION ON THE BODY

One of the best clues for determining how the condition has affected a person, and what issues are still unresolved, is by observing which part of the body is experiencing the condition. Once you identify the location of the condition, you can look up the emotional mind/body connection with that particular area and begin to pray for healing. (See specific details about conditions affecting particular body parts in chapter 15.)

EVERY PART OF YOUR BODY HAS A FUNCTION AND PURPOSE

When there is physical and emotional trauma, the body part may not function as it is expected to until there is a release of the trauma. For example, below you will see that the body location of the spinal column has the major function of supporting the entire body structure. Without the spine, you would not be able to stand or sit up straight. Interestingly, the major emotional influence for the lack of healing to spinal conditions is lack of emotional support. As a result, it is important that you identify past trauma in which the afflicted person did not, or still does not, feel emotionally supported. You can suppress emotion from thirty years in the past, only to have it resurface because of a current event that illicits the same emotion. People often push away (suppress) old hurts and dismiss past feelings by saying things like, "It doesn't bother me anymore" or "I've forgiven them a long time ago." As I mentioned earlier, suppressed past emotion can become a barrier to healing of the current effects of trauma. In addition, even if you *say* you have forgiven someone, you must take the opportunity to properly identify and release the suppressed unhealthy emotion to ensure proper forgiveness from your heart. The following is an example of the emotional connection to the body location and function. (See details in chapter 15.)

Body location	Fuction/Purpose of Body Part	Emotional Connection
Spinal column	Support structure for the body	Lack of emotional support
Shoulders	Carrying loads	Overwhelming stress. The bur of caring for others.
Neck	Structural stability and support for the head	Cannot let feelings out, inflex state of mind. Someone is "a p in the neck!"

2. COMBINE BODY LOCATION AND THE WORDS YOUR HEAR

As you expand your search, listen to the Holy Spirit and combine the location of the condition with the words and feelings you see and hear. This will give you greater clues to what may be blocking the healing. The following case examples will give you some idea how to combine the location and the words.

BACK PAIN

When the afflicted person complains of long-term back pain, you can remember that the spinal column is a major support structure for the body, but its emotional connection is due to lack of emotional support from important people or places (job, school, church, etc.). As a result, you can do the following:

+ Ask the Holy Spirit to reveal any past events or traumas when the condition started.

+ Ask the person if they have ever felt lack of support by an important person or an organization in their past or present.

+ When the person identifies people who did not, or currently do not, provide needed emotional support, have them describe what it felt like to suffer with lack of support (identify the offending people as early in life as possible). Remember, most adults that relate to life as *a victim* or as *helpless* (as earlier stated earlier on p. 123) are exhibiting behavior and feelings learned from the past.

+ If the person cannot recall specific people or places, ask them to picture themselves as a child in their home, and to describe what they think it must have felt like to live there. Ask if they felt emotionally supported growing up.

+ Then go through Step II of the Steps for Healing Prayer.

After I prayed four times for a woman with back pain, there was still no change in her pain. I asked her about forgiveness and she said she needed to forgive her brother for a sexual act when she was a little girl. She also needed to forgive her parents for not protecting her. When she forgave everyone, the pain disappeared. At first thought, you would think the event with her brother had nothing to do with her back pain. However, this woman was carrying feelings of resentment from her experience of not experiencing love and support from her family. Each suppressed hurt blocked her healing.

KNEE AND LEGS

Since the purpose of our legs, knees, and feet is to provide forward mobility, if the afflicted person tells you about feeling *restricted, stuck, unable to move forward in life,* and *helpless to make changes,* chances are, they felt the same way at some point in their past. This usually stems from situations such as having overly strict parents, abusive relationships, or someone having a medical condition. The past unresolved emotion will intensify any emotion felt in present-day circumstances, and create a hindrance to healing. Typically, if the person has lived with these feelings long enough, they may not see the emotional connection with a specific body location, or the connection to a past situation. However, their body is telling them otherwise. Most people put these offenses away, believing they are done with them. You can go through these simple steps:

+ Ask the Holy Spirit to reveal any past unresolved issues.

+ Ask the person about an event, person, or situation that has caused these feelings of helplessness.

+ If they struggle to remember, ask them to describe what it must have felt like to live that way.

+ Go through Step II found in the Steps for Healing Prayer.

SHOULDERS

Pain in the shoulders that does not heal has an emotional connection to carrying the stress and burdens from caring for others, overwhelming situations, dealing with financial difficulties, and an inability to set healthy boundaries with others.

I saw a woman who had suffered from shoulder pain for fifteen years. Prayer and medical treatment had been unsuccessful in easing her pain. When I asked whom she was responsible for, a stressed look appeared on her face as she explained how she had been caring for her mother for the fifteen years since her father had passed away. Over the years, the overwhelming burden had increased her neck and shoulder pain from a past injury. As we prayed, she first released the grief from her father's death, and then she released the false belief that she alone was responsible for the care of her mother. After she had forgiven her mother and herself for taking on the burden and the false belief, her pain automatically disappeared.

1. Ask the Holy Spirit to reveal unresolved issues from the past.

2. Ask the afflicted person about an event, person, or situation that has caused them to take on overwhelming responsibility or burdens.

3. If so, ask the person to describe what it has been like to take on that responsibility.

4. Go through Step II of the Steps for Healing Prayer.

HEAD

When the afflicted person complains of long-term unresolved conditions, such as headaches and migraines, they often feel overwhelmed, experience emotional or mental stress, and have not learned how to deal with pressure and stress. If you take on excessive amounts of responsibility, or if you have difficulty expressing feelings, you are prone to feel overwhelmed and stressed. The longer you have lived with this, the less you will be aware of the impact of your stress level.

1. Ask the Holy Spirit to reveal unresolved issues from the past.

2. Ask the afflicted person whether they are able to freely express feelings, and if they are experiencing stressful situations in their life.

3. Ask them to describe what it has felt like to live that way. The person needs to regularly identify and release their feelings.

4. Go through Step II of the Steps for Healing Prayer.

PUTTING IT TOGETHER WHEN EXPANDING YOUR SEARCH:

As you ask the Holy Spirit for guidance while you are expanding your search, you will more easily be able to combine information about the source of the condition, evaluate the words being expressed, and determine what is blocking the healing. If healing still doesn't happen, expand your search using the following steps:

1. Listen to words and expression of feelings.

2. Observe the location of the condition on the body.

3. Ask about other hindrances that can block healing. (Review chapter 11, Other Hindrances That Can Block Healing.)

4. Consider the location of pain in the body and the words being expressed, and then ask the afflicted person about an event, person, or situation that may have caused or contributed to the feelings they have described. For best results during ministry, simultaneously use Step II and Step V found in chapter 10.

13

HEALING PRAYERS CAN WORK FOR YOU TOO!

Josh herniated a disc in his back when he was a child and then injured his back again while playing sports as a teenager. This caused a bulging disc, which he lived with for many years. When Josh underwent back surgery three years prior, an accident on the operating table caused him to remain in the hospital for months. As a result, he suffered severe physical problems, such as leg weakness below the knees, and the inability to walk, stand, or sit without pain. Prayer and medical treatments had been unsuccessful in his healing, and his emotional and memory traumas had never been addressed. I prayed with Josh as he pictured Jesus with him before, during, and after the surgery, as well as his three months spent in a hospital bed. When I ask God to send away Josh's physical and emotional trauma, his pain level decreased to half of what it had been. When I asked Josh to forgive himself and others for the repeated injuries, his back pain completely disappeared.

I praise God when I see people like Josh become free from a life of illness and suffering. However, I must admit there was a time earlier in my Christian walk when I wondered if God could heal people through my prayers. In fact, if you go back even earlier, I did not even know that Christians were expected to pray for healing. I have come to realize my earlier church experiences were like those of so many people who have never heard or experienced healing prayer. For some, praying for healing was done only by the anointed leaders of God. Since your early experience with healing prayer creates your expectation for healing later in life, the more exposure to the miracles of God you get, the more you will hold on to the belief that miracles are real. However, a common obstacle to healing is a lack of belief that God can heal others through your own prayers.

Remember, the measure of your belief can be determined by the measure of belief someone of greater authority first gave to you. There is a church I know where everyone is taught and encouraged to pray for healing as a way of life. Even the little children have Sunday school classes about the power of healing prayer and are expected to pray for others. I hear about stories like the one about a six-year-old who noticed a man walking with a limp in the church hallway. The boy asked the man if he could pray for his physical condition, and when the boy prayed, the man's condition was healed! Since healing prayer was a normal part of this boy's family and church life, praying and believing for healing was natural. *"And all things you ask in prayer, believing, you will receive"* (Matthew 21:22).

WHEN BELIEVING FOR YOUR HEALING DOES NOT COME EASILY

Like many people, my belief in healing did not come easily. When I was in college, I worked in the school kitchen, leaning over large sinks to scrub pots and pans to help pay for my tuition. After many months, that work took its toll on my back. One night, when I was lifting a heavy pot out of the sink, I felt an intensely sharp pain in my lower back, like someone just stabbed me. I ended up in the local emergency room for treatment. For the next thirty years, I endured back pain on and off, with bouts of excruciating pain that came with a disabling force. I would do the usual routine of doctor visits, bedrest, and pain relievers to get some relief, and I was told to "learn to live with it."

Even though, as a professional, I saw the power of God helping others become healed from emotional pain and suffering, I struggled with why I could not get my own healing. I knew I did not want to live this way, and that I served a powerful God. I later realized that I had never recognized how much my physical condition was impacted by my emotional issues and lack of knowledge about physical healing.

During those years of suffering, I experienced one of those back episodes that produced excruciating pain. Not wanting to disappoint my family, I forced myself to get through family activities. When I was not able to obtain a doctor's appointment before the weekend, my wife and I began praying over my back. At that time, praying was second or third on the priority list of treatments. Even though there was no relief, I finally heard the Lord say, "Wait until Sunday." At that time, we were not part of a church that prayed for healing, so we did not understand what God meant by that. But my wife and I were hungry to see healing miracles and experience more of what God had for us, so we decided to visit a church because the pastors had invited us to attend a few weeks earlier.

Even though my back was in extreme pain, we decided to attend the new church with a sense of anticipation for what God was going to do. At the end of the service, the pastor invited anyone who needed healing prayer to come to the front. We figured it must have been a "God moment," since I did not expect healing prayer during our visit to this church. I struggled to make it to the front with the usual extreme pain that exploded in my lower back and shot down my legs. I held on to each pew as I hobbled slowly down the aisle. Although I thought it was odd, I complied when the prayer team asked me to lie down on the floor. As I struggled to lie down, I was filled with both fear and excitement about what may happen. I knew the Lord could heal, but I had experienced pain for so long, I had doubts about my healing. The prayer ministers gave simple but firm commands for my hips and legs to adjust, and for God to bring healing.

I didn't understand it all, but I was willing to be obedient when they asked me to stand up and test out my back. With my usual caution, I turned onto my side and realized there was no pain. This encouraged me to continue moving, and I stood up with absolutely no pain! At first, I was shocked, then overjoyed, as I tried to process what had just happened. I walked around the sanctuary praising God, as I felt totally healed. After that day, it took me three weeks to transition from the worry of anticipating the pain returning to fully believing that I was completely healed. There were no instructions on how to act like a healthy person, so I had to think back to how I lived life with a healthy back. All along, I kept reading what God said in His Word about healing, and I had to constantly remind myself I was well whenever faced with activities that would have brought pain to my back. Through it all, I realized I still needed to take care of myself, with regular stretching, exercise, and walking, to keep my back strong.

IMPROVING YOUR FAITH TO BELIEVE IN HEALING

After that amazing experience, I took a hard look at my own relationship with God and how I viewed healing prayer. I realized my faith in God was strong, but my belief that He would work through me was weak. It was my own lack of faith that left me struggling to believe what God could do through my prayers. I wanted to believe in Luke 1:37, that nothing is impossible for God. I continued my journey to strengthen my belief with reading the Word, surrounding myself with opportunities for worship, and learning more about healing prayer. However, what helped me most was receiving inner healing ministry for the past issues that created my original struggle to believe. I did not realize that the important people in my past did not give me the attention, love, and affection I needed, which contributed to my struggle to have confidence and belief in myself. When my past hurts were revealed and released, I had room in my heart to actually receive love from the Father. God's love was different from anything I had ever felt before. I moved into a closer relationship with Jesus, which increased my sense of confidence to believe that God was able to heal others through me.

My emotional healing revealed how much God loved me, and how much I meant to Him, in ways I had never experienced before. This experience revealed a central truth: I had *knowledge* that God loved me, but I did not know what real love *felt* like. I realized that I had been unable to fully feel the love of my heavenly Father because I had not first fully experienced the love of my earthly father. And although I had heard messages about, and was intellectually aware of, how to exercise my freedom to pursue and receive the love of God, I always struggled to actually experience it for myself. That is why people can memorize Scripture, attend conferences, and spend time with God in prayer, but still be unable to fully "get there" or "feel" His loving presence. I want to make it clear that doing those activities can and should bring you closer to God, but you can still struggle if you have past, unresolved emotional hurts or traumas that act as barriers, blocking you from experiencing the real love of God. That is why revealing, releasing, and restoring your soul from traumatic wounds is so important.

As I released my soul wounds, I was able to experience His presence in my heart. This allowed me to experience a sense of authority and power that I had never encountered before, and an increased sense of confidence to step out in faith whenever I saw an opportunity for God to heal someone. I strongly recommend anyone who lacks feelings of love, worthiness, and confidence to receive inner healing by releasing the negative feelings and traumas and restoring the love that God wants you to have. You can use the Steps for Healing Prayer for your own healing. It is God's desire that you receive healing and have strong faith to pray for healing in others. You do not need to wait until you have a radical event in your life to increase your faith to believe the impossible is possible with God.

Suggestions for those seeking more of God to receive healing:

+ Pursue your healing, and never stop seeking opportunities for healing prayer.

+ After you receive healing prayer, stand on the promises that you are healed by the blood of Jesus, rather than trusting only what you see or feel. If you struggle to believe you can be healed, seek inner healing for those feelings.

+ Stand on the belief that God is a loving, merciful Father who wants you to be healed. He is not like your earthly father. If you do not feel loved by God, seek inner healing for those feelings.

+ Build up your faith by reading Scripture about healing and God's promises to you.

+ Spend time in worship and pray with like-minded believers who are excited about seeing the miracles of Jesus every day.

+ Remember that God is not angry at you and does not use illness as punishment, judgment, or condemnation against you.

+ Read other miracle stories to gain understanding and encouragement.

+ Do not allow a lack of healing in your past keep you from believing for healing now.

+ Pursue emotional healing through prayer ministers or Christian professionals. Examine your relationship with authority figures, your belief system, and your relationship with God through the process of revealing, releasing, and restoring your spirit, soul, and body.

Suggestions for those seeking more of God to pray for the healing for others:

+ Spend time with God, asking Him to fill your heart with His love, and to build up your understanding and confidence to use His power and authority.

+ Spend time in worship, at healing conferences, and on healing ministry trips.

- Become involved in soaking prayer centers, Bible studies, and praying with like-minded believers who pray, think, and believe in the miracles of Jesus.

- Build your faith by reading Scripture about healing and God's promises for you.

- After you ask God for opportunities, begin to keep an eye out for people who need healing prayer.

- Pursue emotional healing through prayer ministers or Christian professionals. Examine your relationship with authority figures, your belief system, and your relationship with God through the process of revealing, releasing, and restoring your spirit, soul, and body.

Suggestions when you pray for others:

- Do not worry if the afflicted person will be healed. Just pray! Your obligation is to pray; God's obligation is to heal.

- When the afflicted person is healed, give God the glory. If they are not healed, give God the disappointment. You win, either way!

- After you pray, instruct the afflicted person to stand on the promise that God is still in the process of healing, whether or not they see or feel it.

- Healing prayer is not about religion; it is about sharing the love of Jesus through your compassion.

- When you pray, you don't need to use a lot of Scripture (although some is certainly helpful). Simply use the name of Jesus when you command the illness to leave and declare the healing to come.

- You do not need to be an expert in healing prayer to pray with someone. Just pray! Don't worry, the afflicted person doesn't know what you don't know!

14

HOW TO KEEP YOUR HEALING

It is more often the case that someone loses their healing because they do not know how to keep it. When you instruct people how to keep their healing, you will experience an increase in the rate of conditions that remain healed. To keep their healing, they will need to change how they act, think, and do even the simplest things. This may seem basic, but it is an important step to live out healing. Lastly, you can give the following general instructions about keeping their healing. (If you desire a copy to give to others, you can go the *Healing Info* page on my website, Insightsfromtheheart.com and read the article "How to Keep Your Healing.")

God's obligation is to heal you when you ask for healing. Your obligation is to stand in faith, believing you received your healing in faith. In order to keep your healing, here are some very important steps you can follow:

1. Believe your healing by exercising your faith.

That is what Jesus wanted you to know when He said, *"All things for which you pray and ask, believe that you have received them, and they will be granted you"* (Mark 11:24). This is done by thinking and acting in the belief you have been healed through everything you do. The next two to three weeks will be an adjustment period. You will need to think and act as a healthy person and not as you did before as a sick person. For example, if your back or leg were healed, when you stand or walk, focus on walking as a healed person. Walk with normal, straight steps, thinking and believing you are healed, rather than how you walked when you had the physical condition.

2. Focus on being healthy and not on a returning feeling.

Many people lose their healing because, as soon as they feel an ache, their mind begins to focus on the ache, which increases worry that the condition is returning. As soon as they experience small pains, old habits or thoughts of the previous condition return. Stay in your healing by rebuking your pain or thoughts and reclaim your belief that you are healed. For example, if you experience a small ache, you can say, "In the name of Jesus, I send this pain away. I am healed, and I will have nothing to do with this pain. Thank you, Jesus, for my healing." Then go back to thinking about how God healed you, even if the ache is still there.

3. Anything good and new you receive from God will be contested by your old negative thought patterns and by the devil himself.

The devil doesn't want you to have what is good! Healing, or a miracle, is no different. *"Resist the devil and he will flee from you"* (James 4:7), and resist your old ways of thinking. How do you resist these? With your faith in the Word of God, which reminds you to fellowship with likeminded people who believe in miracles (see Romans 1:12), and promises that whatever you receive from God is yours to keep (see Mark 11:24; Luke 6:38; James 1:5; 1 John 2:27). Remember, you are not only battling your sickness; you are also battling a force that does not want you healed. When you pray to send away the pain, therefore, remember that you have already received God's gift of healing, so you can tell the enemy to leave and take the pain with him. Ask your Christian friends to pray with you and help you to keep your thoughts and behaviors healthy by encouraging you when you have negative thoughts.

4. Regularly thank God for your healing and spend time meditating on the Word of God.

The well-known healer, Smith Wigglesworth, once said, "If you wait to build your faith till you need it, it's too late." This is one reason David was able to defeat Goliath, because he had built his faith earlier against both a lion and a bear. That is why you need to regularly thank God for your healing and strength. Spend quality time in the Bible every day, meditating on the Word of God. When you think the way God thinks, you'll see things differently and it will build your faith. There are many Scriptures to encourage your faith about healing. The more you know what the Word of God says about healing, the easier it will be to walk in your healing. I suggest you start by reading Scriptures such as: Matthew 21:22; Mark 16:15–18; John 14:12–14; Luke 1:37; Luke 4:18; 1 Peter 2:24; and James 5:14–15.

15

SUGGESTED EMOTIONAL CONNECTION TO MIND/BODY CONDITIONS

The suppressed emotion resulting from every physical or emotional trauma becomes stored throughout the body, creating a weakened state of functionality. In turn, the body becomes more susceptible to illness, and the stored emotion can interfere with the release of the condition and block healing. One of the best ways to open a pathway for healing to occur is to reveal and release the following emotional barriers to mind/body conditions.

How to use this information for healing:

1. Locate your emotional or physical condition in this chapter, and then identify each of the emotions you have experienced that are listed with that condition. (If a condition is not listed, look up the body part/location affected. The emotional issues will be the same. For example, if you cannot find "cancer of the pancreas," look up "pancreas" instead.)

2. Ask God to take you to a time earlier in your life when you first had these feelings. This will help as you begin using Step II of the Steps for Healing Prayer.

3. Because it may be difficult to identify your own contributing emotions, ask family or friends to help you identify emotions that may apply to your condition.

EMOTIONAL CONNECTIONS TO MIND-BODY CONDITIONS

Abasia (leg impairment): Difficulty thinking straight; easily distracted; afraid things will not work out

Abdomen: Bad judgment (lack of wisdom); identification with possessions; little sense of self; distrustful; possessive of others; worry about others; tension; fear and anxiety; disharmony; trapped/controlling relationships

Abdominal cramps: Distrustful; stuck; tension; fear of the future; overly responsible; raised in a dysfunctional family; can't move forward

Abscesses: Seething; unresolved hurt; desire for revenge

Acid reflex: Fear of abandonment; restrictive; suppressed emotions; fear of the future

Accident-prone: Intense stress; tension and worry; resistant to authority; defenseless; need to self-punish; unable to take a stand; wishy-washy; afraid of being in the wrong place

Aches: Loneliness; unloved; ache to be held and loved; rebuked and thwarted; sadness

Acne: Guilt, self-rejection/dislike of self; in denial of unpleasant realities; unwilling to face issues

ADD, ADHD (see Attention Deficit Disorder)

Addictions: Disapproval of self; self-rejection; despair; inability to think/perceive clearly or correctly; running from self; void in the soul; avoids feelings; unloved; unsatisfied, impulsive

Addison's disease: Lack of self-understanding; self-anger; inability to understand emotions; unmerciful toward self

Adenoids: Disharmony in the home; restricted; raised without acceptence or with hostility; unwelcome; in the way

Adrenal problems: Feel like a victim; defeated; ambivalent; anxiety; misuse of the will; believe life must have burdens; unresolved jealousy and fear; struggle is necessary for success, power, or position

Aging problems: Inability to accept present circumstances; fear of self; long-standing and unresolved negative feelings

AIDS: Defenseless; hopeless; uncared for; unworthiness; self-denial; deep-rooted anger

Alcoholism: Inability to cope; futility; ambivalent; worthlessness; self-rejection; living a lie; guilt, inadequacy; unresolved negative emotions; believing the negative words of others; defensiveness toward emotions

Allergies: Suppressed emotions, especially tears; resistant to change; fear of expressing emotion; stifled; deny own power

Allergies (environmental): Obsessed with taking charge; irritation; anxiety; repressed emotions; overreract to people; rejection; undeserving of love; no expectation of love; unexpressed grief and despair

Alzheimer's disease: Tired of coping; can't face life anymore; out of control; inferiority; insecure; suppressed anger; lives in own little world; hopelessness and helplessness

Amnesia: Inability be assertive or stand up for self; desire to escape problems or run away; fear of the future

Anemia: Anger at self for inability to control things; dissatisfaction with life direction; not good enough; manipulative, but resentful at being manipulated; joylessness; disordered life

Anemia (pernicious): Helplessness; want to give up; unresolved grief

Aneurysm: Narcissistic; rescuer; unmet needs; repressed; resentful; raised in dysfunctional/blaming family

Ankles: Fear of falling or failing; inflexibility; unstable in challenging situations; difficulty moving forward in life

Ankles (swollen): Overworked; trapped; stuck; can't quit; can't find relief from pressures in life

Anorectal bleeding: Anger; frustration about most things in life

Anorexia: Unable to please a parent (usually mother), unable to live up to expectations, self-rejection, self-hatred

Anus: Survival is threatened by outside conditions; powerless in some area of life

Anxiety (see also panic attacks and separation anxiety): Uable to "call the shots" in life; helpless to affect change; lack of control; past unresolved trauma

Apathy: "Spark of life" has gone out; numb; resistant to emotions; cannot feel

Aphasia: Difficulty forming words; opinions not valued; seen but not heard; afraid to say the wrong thing

Appendicitis: Fearful about life; unable to deal with fear; low energy

Appetite (loss of): Incorrect perceptions of others; distrustful; depression; excessively unloved, unaccepted, or unprotected

Arm problems: Difficulty holding on to life experiences; trouble grasping ideas; difficulty upholding convictions or perceptions of what you should be doing; anxiety/fear of underachievement

Arteries (hardening): Fear of disappointment; hardhearted; dictatorial; desires obstructed or delayed in life; unresolved feelings obscure productivity

Arteriosclerosis: Inability to express feelings/emotions; unable to see the positive; unresolved negative emotions; refusal to be open-minded

Arthritis: Critical of self or others; holds on to hostility; holds on to negative beliefs; long-term resentment; anger; bitterness; long-term anxiety and/or depression; supressed anger; need to be right;

rigid thinking/feeling; uncompromising; inflexibility; inability to express anger

Arthritis (degenerative joint disorder or DJD): Self-criticism; unworthiness; fear; anger; restricted and confined; underperforming due to self-doubt and fear; unloved; resentment; bitterness; judgmental; blaming and critical, lack of love and rejection in childhood and beyond; suppressed feelings

Arthritis (rheumatoid): Body receives conflicting messages; worthlessness; laughing outside/crying inside; helplessness; overwhelmed

Asthma: Relive childhood fears; need for dependence; chronic anxiety and fear; unconscious dependency wishes; dominated by a parent; unable to protest unjust treatment; overly sensitive; suppressed sorrow/crying; stifled

Athlete's foot: Unaccepted; fear of being unfit; raised with conditional love; not good enough; stuck in place; inability to move forward; fear of failure; self-disapproval; agitated

Attachment disorder: Issues of abandonment; afraid to get hurt; difficulty with trust; fear of people leaving; fear of being alone; fear of loss; past hurts from important people; uncared for; past unresolved trauma

Attention Deficit Disorder (ADD; same as "racing mind"): Mind does not stop; life out of control; made to feel stupid or "less than"; difficulty fitting in; not feeling good about self; not allowed to think for self; must prove self; mother was anxious during pregnancy, causing exhausted adrenal gland; past trauma, fear, and chaos

Attention Deficit Hyperactivity Disorder ADHD (same as ADD with addition of these symptoms): Cannot slow down; fear of missing something; cannot keep up; confusion, nervous; fear of bad things happening; worried; anxious from hypervigilance from past/present trauma/chaos

Autoimmune system: Laughing on outside/crying on inside; inability to deal with life; responsible for ills/burdens of others; long-term accululated and suppressed emotions destroying self inside; deep grief/despair

Back problems: Lack of emotional support; emotional difficulties; burdened emotionally; frustration; desire for people to "get off my back"

Back problems (lower): Unsupported financially; money concerns; desire to back out of commitment; hurtful relationship; desire to run away from a situation

Back problems (middle): Guilt; lacking self-support and confidence

Back problems (upper): Unsupported or burdened emotionally; frustration; withholding love from others; agitated or anxious

Bad breath: Unfinished; unsatisfied solutions in life; raised in dysfunctional, unavailable family

Balance problems: Disorientation in life; thrown off base; at risk and confused in potentially dangerous world; poor sense of direction; tired of demands and responsibilities

Bedwetting: Fear; rejection; unworthiness; anger; lack of control over situation; anxiety; distrust of self/others

Bell's palsy (facial paralysis): Unwilling to express self; fear of losing self-control; judgmental toward self; internal anger; raised in invasive and oppressive family

Bipolar: Unsettled; unorganized; ungrounded; out of control; need for control; stressed out; easily overwhelmed; unsettled since the womb

Bladder problems: Fear; peeved; stifled; anger; timidity; need for approval; lack of control; ineffective; inefficient; weary/tired; repressed sexual feelings; inharmonious relationships; unexpressed sexual identity; desire for order; overly concerned with survival issues (money, job, health); inability to release things no longer needed

Bleeding gums: Inability to feel joy over decisions

Blindness: Overwhelmed; hard to deal with life; unresolved fear; desire to run away

Blisters: Emotionally unprotected; resistant to flow of life; unsafe

Blood clots: Intensely conservative; restrictive; resistant to change; difficulty experiencing joy; dealt with difficult changes in childhood

Blood disorders: Powerless in some area of life; deep anger; long-standing ill will; intense depression

Blood problems: Joylessness; stagnant thinking; unable to go with life's flow; fear

Blood problems (low platelets): Overly responsible; poor limit-setting or self-care

Blood pressure (high): Pressured; endangered; depressed; resentment; powerless; surpressed emotions; overly self-reliant; inability to relax

Blood pressure (low): Defeated; resentment; unloved; anxiety; unsafe

Blurred vision: Difficulty accepting what eyes see; difficulty focusing; raised in demoralizing dysfunctional family; unaccepting of realities

Boils: Boiling over with anger inside; deprived; resentful; betrayed; sabotaged in life; denied love and joy as a child

Bones (broken): Separation/disconnected feelings; life seems obstinate or fixed

Borderline disorder: Impulsive; insecure; mood swings; difficulty with trust and love; difficulty with intimacy; paranoid about what people say; easily upset; raised in unstable, neglectful, distrustful, hurtful, unloving home

Bowels: Fear of displeasing others, controlling; fearful of not having enough; fearful of lack of control; possessiveness; fearful of releasing old ideas that are no longer useful

Brain problems: Nervousness; anxiety; lack of control; drained; over-demanding; worrying

Brain tumor: deep mental conflict; withdrawn; confusion; disoriented; devastated about life; pessimistic; stubborn about changing ways; rigid in views about life; raised in strict, rigid childhood environment

Breasts: Conflicted about worthiness; denies self-worth; conflicted about nurturing ability

Bronchitis: Disharmony in the home; anger; anxiety; withholds emotions; afraid of self-expression; afraid; tense; helpless

Bruises: Need to self-punish; self-rejecting, victim mentality; at risk in the world; raised in an accusing environment

Bulimia: Mistaken self-image; self-rejecting; lacks self-control; dissatisfied; unmet needs; self-contempt; unable to measure up to others; raised in controlling, restricted home

Bunions: Constant fear

Bursitis: Anxiety; repressed anger; not in control; helpless to change a situation; tense; violent urges; frustrated

Calluses: Inability to flow with life; antisocial; resists learning new things

(For specific cancer not found below, look up the body location in this chapter)

Cancer (blood/leukemia): Depression, anger or ill will

Cancer (cervix): Repressed anger

Cancer (female organs):   Repressed anger (usually at male authority); emptiness; unresolved resentment, suppressed hostility; self-rejecting; despair; repressed loneliness; poor relationship with parents; inability to cope with loss; hopelessness/helplessness; repression; depression; hate, vengeance, or jealousy; resists divine/spiritual help; lacking desire to live

Cancer (melanoma): Frustrated; irritated by others; hurt and resentment; profound grief; hateful thoughts; unforgiveness; withholds emotions; deep disappointment; unable to feel loved; anger

Cancer (multiple myeloma): Tormented by secrets or grief; harboring hurt, bitterness, or resentment; burdened; silent suffering; surpressed feelings

Cancer (small of back): Inner strife with happy mask; heavy burdens; unresolved emotions

Cancer (stomach): Condemnation; hateful thoughts; spiteful feelings of malice; desire for revenge; unforgiveness

Cancer (uterus): Easily irritated by others; anger; feeling like a martyr

Candida: Roiling inner resentment; blames others; powerlessness; unresolved negative feelings

Canker sores: Unresolved negativity; overworked; emotional stress; emotional pain; anxious over details

Car sickness: Fear of the world; trapped in bondage; subconscious rage

Carpal tunnel: Life is unfair; powerlessness; wronged or sense of injustice

Cardiovascular disorder: Agitated; impatient; driven to compete and achieve; low self-esteem; want matters to move more quickly

Cataracts: Gloomy/afraid of the future; helplessness; lack of control over events; avoids looking to future

Cerebral palsy: Paralyzed thought life, make everything right; overly responsible; guilt; rejection; inability to let go or forgive

Chest: Unprotected at belief and emotional core; unprotected; unresolved fear; lack of approval or self-love; powerlessness; rejected and hurt in love

Cholesterol: Undeserving of happiness; denies self of joy

Chronic diseases: Distrust; unsafe; avoids risk; unwilling to change for better

Chronic fatigue syndrome: Despair; desolation; loneliness; despondant; hopelessness; lacking will to live; low self-worth

Circulation problems: Overloaded; job disatisfaction; stuck at job; tension and discouragement; constant need to prove self

Codependency: Fear of being alone; fear of failure; unloved; abandonment issues; dependent on others for source of happiness

Colds: Unkind feelings toward others; confusion in home and in life; belief in seasonal sicknesses

Cold sores (fever blisters): Surpressed anger; pressured or burdened by responsibility; unable to cope with pressure; resentful of burdens

Colic: Unhappy with surroundings; irritation and impatience; annoyance/emotional tension from parents and/or surroundings

Colitis (also see colon problems): Overly concerned with order; fear of losing freedom; excessive worry; oppression and defeat; desire for more affection

Colitis (ulcerative): Obsessive-compulsive behavior; indecisive; anxiety; surpressed hostility or anger; need to conform; feeling like a martyr

Colon problems: Difficulty processing/handling issues; inability to let go; holds on to past, unresolved hurts; suppressed hated; burdened; emotional issues; suppressed grief and emotional reactions

Conjunctivitis: Easily frustrated; anger; overly critical

Congestive heart failure: Rejection; abandonment; unloved; isolation; hopelessness; broken-hearted from issues in the past

Constipation: Worried; anxious; hesitant to move forward in life; unwilling to release unhealthy feelings and beliefs; unresolved problems

Conversion disorder: Immaturity; resistant to growing up; demanding; avoids responsibility or accountability; treated as a child by others

Corns: Holding on to past hurts; hard feelings; overly focused on the past

Coughs: Nervousness; obsessed by negative thoughts; overly critical; easily annoyed; choking sensation

Cramps: Fear of pain; refusal to move forward; stubbornly holds incorrect perceptions of femininity, built-up tension; negative experiences as child

Crohn's disease: Lack of good discernment; insecure; not good enough; distrust; undeserving; deprived in life; not valued by others; self-disapproving

Cysts: Sorry for self, inability to resolve hurt feelings, guilt-based self-rejection, raised in blaming/shaming family

Cystic fibrosis: Belief that "life works for everyone else, but not me"; chronic grief; depression; joy-avoidant; unworthy of living a full life

Cystitis: Unresolved irritability; unhappy thought patterns

Deafness: Not wanting to hear what is going on; poor self-worth; desire for isolation; lack of self-love; live in own little world

Defiant behavior/thinking: Unloved; abandoned; betrayed; rejection; unwanted; not special; unsupported; unappreciated; singled out for criticism; defiant behavior becomes means of attracting attention

Degenerative joint disease (DJD; see arthritis)

Delirium: Repressed or suppressed desires or fears; repressed memories coming to the surface; raised in oppressive or denial-dominated home

Dementia: Hopeless and helpless; tired of constantly struggling; unresolved anger; bitterness and disgust; anger and resentment; raised in uncaring, demanding, and/or unloving home

Depression: Apathetic about life; discouragement; hopelessness; pessimism; guilt; worthlessness; helplessness; suppressed anger; not good enough; unsupported; emptiness of heart; frequently hurt; unresolved hurts and disappointments

Dermatitis (see Skin)

Deviated septum: Keep nose out of people's business; unsure of role in life; overly inquisitive mind; conflicted about life; afraid to rock the boat

Diabetes: Overly critical of self or others; disappointment; chronic sorrow; emotional shock; lack of joy; "life should have been different"; obsessed with control

Diarrhea: Rejecting what you can't accept; wanting to be done with someone or something; running away from a situation; obsessed with order; fear of something in the present

Dissociative identity disorder (multiple personality): Distrust; fear of being hurt; no one is safe; on guard; hyper vigilance; life is scary and unpredictable; unsafe; withdrawn/don't let others close; distant; unresolved past trauma

Diverticulitis: Self-punishing; self-deprivation; rejection; past guilt; unrealistic expectations; self-recrimination

Dizziness: Overloaded, can't cope; unaccepting of reality; unresolved anger; built-up resentment; unnecessarily takes on burdens of others

Dowager's hump: Unresolved anger; built-up resentment; unnecessarily takes on burdens of others

Drop foot: Afraid to take action, cause trouble, or move forward; overly conservative; afraid to betray basic values and beliefs

Dropsy (fluid in the abdomen): Not letting go; resistant to change; obsessed with the past; fear of bad things happening; avoids change; carrying burdens; afraid to ask for help; afraid of alienating and losing support; afraid of losing love

Dry eye: Inability to express grief; emotionally distant or dead; holds incorrect perceptions from the past; unable to cry

Duodenum problems: Unmet dependency needs, loneliness; neglected; overwhelmed by futility of life; raised in neglectful and depriving home

Dysentery: Fears; unjust treatment; oppressed; endangered; powerlessness; general lack of authority or control; raised in indifferent or hostile home

Dyslexia: Unplanned or unwanted in utero; abandoned or neglected as infant or child; lack of stimulation and development to connect to world

Dysmenorrhea: Self anger; inability to forgive self

Dystonia: Fear of consequences; afraid to succeed as a child; fear of bad things happening; fear of hurting others

Ear (*hearing corresponds with ability to understand*)

Ear (hearing problems): Want people to hear things your way; despair; denied or humiliated; undermined; rage; conflict adverse

Ear (inner ear): Aggravated; poor decision-making; life redirection

Ear (ringing): Noise trauma; overwhelmed inside; inner belief of not being good enough

Earache: Anger at what you hear; don't want to hear what is going on

Earache (children): Can't abide turmoil in the home

Eating disorder: Fear of losing control; bad feelings about self; need to be perfect; see yourself as ugly; past unresolved trauma; unloved; neglected; judged by others; not good enough; view other people as too controlling

Eczema: Overly sensitive; unresolved hurt feelings; prevented from doing something; interrupted in doing something; frustration; unresolved irritation

Edema: Sympathy for self; don't want to move too fast; body's way of immobilizing itself; unnecessarily holding on to something

Elbow: Inability to accept new experiences or to change focus; resists achievement or confidence; fear of demands of others; taken advantage of

Elimination problems: Subconscious resentments; hold on to past experiences; can't let things go; built-up blockages and tension

Emotionless: Afraid to express emotions; not understood; not allowed to speak mind; feelings are not good enough; past trauma unresolved

Emphysema: unworthy to live; fear to live life to the fullest

Endocrine system: Imbalance; out of control; raised in chaotic dysfunctional family

Endometriosis: Deep-seeded unresolved sadness; frustration; insecurity; lack of self-love; blame problems on others

Energy depletion (lack of): Unresolved sadness; tired of the daily struggle; wishing you could quit, depression, despair, demoralization

Epilepsy: Overwhelmed; self-persecuting; desire to reject present life; self-harming; overly burdened; resentful; can't meet expectations

Epstein-Barr virus: Unfulfilled use of gifts; despair and rage; mental and emotional distress; controlled by others; no sense of purpose and direction; self-rejection

Esophagus problems: Indecisiveness over whether or what to eat; distrust; rejection; food issues early in life

Estrogen problems: Conflicted about femininity/identity; rejection; feeling unfeminine; easily influenced

Eyes (bloodshot): Excessive pressure; overworked; fatigue; processing deep issues; conflict with inner feelings

Eyes (circles under): Bitterness; remorse/regret; self-condemnation; deep-seeded grief; unfulfillment; resentment/hurt

Eyes (cornea): Longstanding hurts; deprivation in childhood; emotions push through to consciousness

Eyes (detached retina): Raised in dysfunctional, denial-dominated home; family standards distorted sense of clarity

Eyes (dry): Out of touch with feelings; emotionally dead from past hurts

Eyes (pink eye): Outraged indignation; can't see what happens around you

Eyes (watery): Inability to express inner grief; can't see the truth; refusal to understand what is seen; fear of the future; refusal to see life as it is; life seems weak and out of focus; not seeing eye to eye with others; unforgiving; inability to see one's self-worth

Face (*deals with identity*)

Face (forehead): Reaction to recent conscious thoughts

Face (paralysis): Harsh self-judgment; self-criticism; rejection; fear; anxiety; doubts about competence; inability to face someone or something; fear of "losing face"; relationship problems

Face (tics): Repressed anger/rage; fear; anxiety; afraid to be seen for who you are

Fainting: Fear of the present; inability to cope; "blanking out" life; powerlessness

Fallopian tubes (blockage): Long-term nervous tension; high-strung temperament; agitation; overreaction

Farsightedness: Suppressed anger; outward focused in life

Fast thinking (racing mind): Mind will not stop; "my life has been taken from me"; stupid, inadequate; less than; inability to fit in; self-critical; can't think for self; need to prove self

Fat (overweight/obesity): Need for protection; resistant to forgiving; supressed anger

Fatigue: Resisting life; bored; unsatisfied with place in life; job or relationship "burn out"

Fear of enclosed spaces (claustrophobia): Fears lack of control; afraid bad things will happen; no control of situation; overly emotional; unresolved past trauma

Fear of relationship commitment: Discouragement; unwillingness to get too close; fear of being emotionally hurt; unresolved abandonment, disappointment, or rejection

Feet: Fear of the future; fear of moving forward in life; failure to understand many aspects of life

Feet: (flat feet): Poor boundaries; vulnerable; unprotected; avoid commitments; insecure

Female health problems: Emotional block regarding sexuality; inadequacies in sexual role; fear or guilt about sex; refuses to "let go" of past; rejects feminine nature; emotionally blocked by mate

Fever: Unable to express anger; resistant; anger "burning up" within; irritated by lack of order; holds on to the past

Fibroid tumors and cysts: Ego has been injured; unexpressed/unresolved hurts and/or guilt; shame; inner confusion; past hurts; rejection

Fibromyalgia: Exhaustion; must perform to be good enough; need to be perfect; fear of what others think; distrust; guilt; self-denial; stuck; past trauma; withholds thoughts and feelings; victim mentality

Finger: Difficulty dealing with details of life; limited imagination; limited inspiration and creativity; fear of loss; tries too hard; poor direction-making; concerned about social standing

Finger (index): Affected by fear and resentment

Finger (little): Affected by pretense, deceit, and unforgiveness

Finger (middle): Affected by anger, bitterness, and sexuality

Finger (ring): Affected by grief, inability to deal with details of life

Finger (thumb): Worry; depression; hateful thoughts; anxiety; guilt; self-protection

Fingernails: Anxiety; perfectionism; avoids change; unprotected; indifference or apathy; raised in unstable home

Fingernails (biting): Desire for self-destruction; resistant to authority; over-analyze tiny details

Flu: Fear; extremely negative; weak and helpless; pessimism (believes the worst will happen); internally conflicted; susceptibility to suggestion

Foot problems: Fear of future; stuck; afraid to take risks; fear of making mistakes; fear of the unknown; unsupported; inability to "stand on their own two feet"; burdened; poor foundation/footing in life; avoids commitment

Frigidity: Unresolved fear; resentment; fixation; guilt regarding sex and sexual relationships; personality issues affecting emotional expression

Fungus: Inability to let go of the past; self-defeating; ruled by the past; insecure; need for constant validation

Gallbladder: Resentment; gall; stubborn; hopeless; incapable; depressed; bitter; angry; desire to force will

Gallstones: Bitterness and condemnation; unyielding; unforgiving; prideful; withdrawn; depressed; unresolved grief

Gangrene: Extreme morbidity; "poisonous" emotions; lack of self-love; insecurity

Gastritis: Uncertainty; anxiety; catastrophic thoughts; dread

Giardia lamblia (intestinal parasites): Undeserving or unimportant; inadequate; not good enough; rejected; deprived; believes expectations of others are unrealistic

Glandular problems: Long-term inappropriate feelings; unresolved emotions have created gross imbalance

Glaucoma: Hostility; unforgiveness; bitterness; unresolved hurts; disappointment; refuses to look to the future; unable to love

Gluten sensitivity: Overly responsible since childhood; overwhelmed; sorrow; grief; despair; rejected as a child

Goiter: Unfulfilled; feel used; life purpose thwarted; powerlessness; poor self-worth; rage; resentment; oppressive childhood

Gout: Judges others harshly; impatient; desire to dominate; suppressed anger; rejects others and the world

Granulocytopenia: Worthless; not good enough

Grave's disease: Driven to excel; perfectionism; undeserving of love; anger from rejection; unloved as a child

Growths: False sense of pride; anger; resentment; unwilling to accept divine help; suppressed hurts; spiritual understanding and values out of balance

Gum problems: Lack of joy or fulfillment; fear of failure; grief; internally conflicted; indecisive; helplessness; vulnerable; insufficient at nurturing

Hair loss: Not free to be self; undeserving of acceptance; feel unfit and worthless

Hand problems: Disappointed by lack of opportunity; manipulated; guilt over outcomes/decisions; anxiety; fear of failure; difficulty with life details; fear of moving forward

Hand problems (arthritis): Rigid; perfectionism; controlling; overly critical of self and others; inflexible; suppressed emotions mirrored in the hands

Hand problems (cramps): Conflicted with abilities; poor communicator; difficulty with verbal communication

Hand problems (left): Difficulty receiving; passivity

Hand problems (right): Difficulty giving; aggressive; fear new ideas; lack of opportunity; difficulty moving forward

Hand problems (sweaty): Fear of making mistakes; incompetent; feel foolish

Hay fever: Unresolved rage or fear; grief; sadness; repressed tears; repressed aggression; desire for vengance; guilt

Headaches: Tense; stress; unresolved emotions; unexpressed hurts; inner pressure; lack of control; overwhelming fear and anxiety; unhealthy relationships; unwillingness to face realities; inability to laugh, sing, praise, or express gratitude

Headaches (cluster): Guilt; fear; failure; unable to relax or trust; resists moving forward; internal clock out of sync; resentment and anger; overly responsible since childhood

Hearing problems (see Ears)

Heart problems: Imbalanced joy; lack of emotion; lack of compassion; rejection; resentment and/or hurt; disapproval of others; difficult family problems; unforgiving of others and self; resists responsibility; hurtful relationship

Heart problems (fibrillation): Loneliness; isolated; cut off

Heart problems (heart murmur): Unloved; ambivalent reception in the womb

Heel: Loneliness; unloved; rejection; overly responsible; unsupported; out of step with life; deserving of bad things

Hemophilia: Hard to set boundary or say "no"; unmet needs

Hemorrhoids: Long-term perception of being burdened; pressured; anxious; fear or tension; inability to let go

Hepatitis: Resistant to change; resentful; anger; fear; self-doubt; highly demanding; controlling childhood; powerless

Hernia: Anger; burdened; self-punishing; emotionally unavailable; unresolved hurt from past relationships

Herpes: Guilt; shame; anxiety; anger; self-rejecting

Herpes (simplex): Unsupported; bitterness; resentful; loneliness; sexual guilt; afraid to speak up

Hiatal hernia: Judgmental; resentful; burdened; discontentment with current circumstances

Hips: Fear of decision-making; pessimistic; fear of the future; power imbalance in home; unsupported; nothing to look forward to

Hips (hip joint): Refusal to accept present circumstances; in denial of physical experiences

Hives: Small hidden fears; resurfacing fear; mistreated; inability to view things with the correct perspective; anger; irritated with inflexible behavior of others; inability to speak up for self

Hoarding: Abandonment issues; unloved; emptiness; sadness; unfulfilled; grief; difficulty finding happiness; fear of losing everything; searching for identity, purpose, and intimacy; unresolved past loss

Hodgkin's disease: Desire for acceptance; not good enough; self-rejecting; need to prove self; joylessness

Huntington's disease: Resentment; need to change others; hopelessness; helplessness; sorrow; fear of failure

Hyperactivity: Needy; lack of peace; needs unmet; agitation; pressure to perform; inability to meet expectations

Hyperglycemia: Rescuer; no time for self; high expectations

Hypertension: (see blood pressure)

Hyperthyroidism: Overly responsible; fear of being unloved; undeserving; left out; rejection; raised in rejecting family

Hyperventilation: Distrust the flow of life; fear of life's uncertainties

Hypoglycemia: Overwhelmly burdened, joylessness

Hypothalamus: Rage; insecurity; displeasure; sadness; anxiety

Hypothyroidism: Giving up; hopelessness; defeated; pessimism; stifled by others

Ileitis: Not good enough; self-disapproval; insecurity; fear of the future; helpless to improve circumstances, especially in childhood

Ileocecal valve: Rigid; self-destructive; can't let go of past; bitterness; raised in authoritarian home

Immune system: Giving up; inability to care for others; out of control; apathetic; persecuted; running on empty; overly responsible since childhood

Impetigo: Singled out and blamed; helplessness/trapped in situations; driven to please others; high expectations; anger

Impotence: Conflicting ideas about sex, fear, resentment; fears toward mother; psychic obsessions or sexual frustration; guilt having to do with sex and sexual relationships

Inability to absorb nutrients: Self-rejection; distrust; pessimism; anticipates disappointment

Incontinence: Need to control emotions; overwhelming emotions

Incurable disease: Long-standing condemnation of self and others; unresolved issues and unforgiving of people and situations in the past

Indigestion: Everyone is against you; disharmony; must fight for everything; insecure; inadequate; resentment; anxiety; fear of losing job and security; feel persecuted

Infection: Hostility/anger; suspicious; annoyed; resentful; inner conflict

Infertility: Fear; tension/conflict/trauma; self-distrust; anxiety; detatchment; harsh; inner turmoil about being a parent; present circumstances not appropriate for child; personal/marital problems

Inflammation: Rage; anxiety; irritated/upset by others; disgust; self-distrusting and disapproving; raised in an unstable home

Influenza: Believe the worst will happen; pessimism

Injuries: Guilt; deserve to be punished; self-anger; deserve to suffer

Insanity: Unable to let go of the past; desire to escape; withdrawn; inability to cope; desire to flee from family

Insomnia: Tension; guilt; fear of letting go; anxiety; fear of threatening situations; inability to trust or love self or others

Intestinal diseases: Inability to assimilate; lives in the past; desire to remain in comfort zone; constipation

Intestinal diseases (intestinal cramps): Difficulty moving forward in life; distrustful

Irritable bowel syndrome (IBS or spastic colon): Insecure; uncared for; unsupported now or in the past; can't let go or flow with life; need to be in control

Itching: Unfulfilled desires; wanting more out of life; unaccepting of current circumstances; intimacy issues; sorrow and regret over the past; sexual guilt; easily irritated

Jaundice: Unloved; disappointed; discouraged; disgusted; resentment; lack of recognition and nurturing

Jaw problems: Rage, wanting revenge, unsafe feelings, can't express feelings, can't make difference in world, resentment

Jaw problems (TMJ syndrome): Surpressed anger; distrust; anxiety; frustrated with life; unrealistic expectations

Joints: Resentment; suppressed hurt; resistant of change; distrust; inflexibile; fear of the future

Kidney problems: Fear; dread; lack of control; overly judgmental; insensitive; emotional confusion; paralyzed will; hostility; obsessive; deep resentment toward people and experiences of the past; unfounded criticism of others; shame, overly contemplative

Kidney problems (kidney stones): Anger; negative thinking; suppressed emotions; unable to get close; unable to meet demands; often blamed in childhood

Knee problems: Resistant toward authority; stubborn; distrustful; ego/pride issues; demand things done your way; fear of failure; unmet needs

Knee problems (knee cap): Difficulty with change; difficulty reaching destiny; won't conform to others

Knee problems (Left): Insecure; unresolved stress

Knee problems (Right): Unassertive, not wanting to *give in* to authority

Lactic acidosis: Family taboos; social restrictions; moral inhibitions; unexpressed passions; suppressed emotions; lack of freedom

Lactose intolerance: Rejected by mother; inadequacy; self-rejecting; not good enough; received harmful messages since childhood

Large intestine: Anxiety; perfectionist; defensive; unloved; abandonment and rejection issues; financial worry; self-defeating; controls emotions; overly responsible

Laryngitis: Fear speaking up; resentful toward authority; unemotional; fear; anger; easily irritated

Left side of body issues: Feminine side; unprotected; unreceiving; irritated by people who talk too much

Leg problems: Fear of moving ahead in life; resists change; indecisive; wishy-washy; inability to understand; unsupported; abandonment issues

Leg problems (paralysis): Avoids unpleasant situations; avoids fearful situations

Leukemia: Depression; anger or ill will; loss of a loved one; loss of job; helplessness; giving up; suppressed emotions, present/future conditions are intolerable; despair

Leukorrhea: Sexual guilt; powerlessness; anger toward mate

Liver: Unresolved anger; irrational; frustration; unforgiveness; resentment and pettiness; judgmental; critical thoughts; unforgiving of self and others; consumed by notions of injustice and revenge; self-condemming; possessive; regretful of the past; sadness

Lock jaw: Rage; desire to control; suppressed emotions

Lou Gehrig's Disease (ALS): Denial of self-worth; denial and/or unaccepting toward success; distrustful of own abilities

Lungs: Unresolved grief and loss; sadness; lack of approval; unappreciated; hurt by loved one; life is monotonous; lack of clarity of thought; anguish; resistant to love

Lungs (pleurisy): Resentment, codependent, unloved, unsupported

Lupus: Grief; giving up; self-rejecting; resentful; laughing on outside/crying on inside; not good enough

Lyme disease: Overly responsible; fear abandonment; overburdened; self-condemning; depressed; trapped; not good enough; rasied with conditional love

Lymph system: Lack of enthusiasm; unaccepted; unemotional; unloved; inadequacy; lack of motivatation; difficulty caring for own needs; shame, raised in shame-based home

Lymphatic vessels: Lack of peace; joylessness; resentful; hatred or anger; raised in unloving, unsupportive home

Malaria: Feel unsafe; distrustful; loneliness; disconnected

Male health problems: Inadequacy fulfilling sexual role; refusing to let go; guilt over infidelity or promiscuity; haunted by unpleasant memories of previous relationships; unfulfilled in love

Mastoiditis: No desire to hear what is being said; fears that affect understanding; feel left out

Memory problems: Undergoing transformation; avoidance/denial of past trauma; powerlessness; desire to forget the past

Meniere's disease: Disorientated; thrown off base; too many responsibilities; poor sense of direction; fear of risk

Meningitis: Unaccepted; self-rejection; anger; blamed by others

Menopause: Fear of getting older; unwanted; rejected; useless; unloved; not good enough; lack of purpose

Menstrual problems: Guilt; self-rejection; disapproval; fears role as a woman; no joy in being a woman

Migraine headaches: Unable to move forward in life; overwhelmed; desire to move at own pace; dislikes being pushed; anger; inability to handle pressure or stress; desire to control, suppressed emotions

Mind: Over analyzes; fear of the unknown

Miscarriage: Fear bad timing; fear what future will bring; fear responsibility for infant; lack of peace with self or mate

Mononucleosis: Unloved and unworthy; difficulty setting limits; anger at being underappreciated; tired of pressure and demands; suppressed emotions; unable to express self

Motion sickness: Fear of not being in control; desire to take charge

Mouth problems: Resistant to change; disappointment and disgust at being unsupported; unable to express self; closed-minded; fear of leaving comfort zone; negative experiences

Multiple chemical sensitivity: Fear of separation; loneliness; vulnerable; distrustful; difficulty letting others in; suppressed emotion; stifled; disappointment; bitterness; unforgiveness; unmet needs; lack of purpose and direction

Multiple sclerosis: Inflexible; unreceptive to new ideas; self-blaming; unforgiving; rigid; resentful of others being irresponsible or unsupporting; suppressed emotions; fear of emotions; self-immobilization creating muscular atrophy

Muscle cramps: Stubbornness, unsafe, resists moving forward, suppressed emotions, "holds on" to emotions, situations, and ideas

Muscular dystrophy (muscular skeletal diseases): Deterioration of emotional strength, causing lack of discernment; self-doubt; anxiety; overwhelmed; hard to move forward; anger; success-avoidance; raised in passive-aggressive home

Myasthenia gravis: Laughing outside/crying inside; helplessness to change conditions; deep-seeded grief; wants to give up; fears change

Nail-biting: Unfulfilled desires; spiteful toward parents; frustration

Narcissistic personality: Inflexible; poor relationship skills; abandonment; unhealthy preoccupation with getting needs met; fear

Narcolepsy: Wishing to be somewhere else; can't cope; weary of responsibility

Nausea: Rejecting unpleasant realities; regret for undesirable situation; fear of something bad happening

Nearsightedness: Childhood fear; sees situations differently

Neck problems: Under pressure; desire to let feelings out but don't dare; inflexible state of mind; unacceptance/rejection of others; irritation with others who are a "pain in your neck"; refusal to yield to opinions you think are wrong

Nephritis: Disappointment; feelings of failure; unfairness of life

Nerves: Surpressed emotions/thoughts; can't let go of the past; distrustful; controlling

Nervous breakdown: Surpressed emotions; fear of the future; powerlessness; uncomfortable with feelings; self-centered; anxious; disappointed; withdrawn; tense; inability to cope

Nervousness: Inability to communicate feelings adequately; fear of the future; anxiety; confused thinking

Neuritis: Easily irritated; power negated because of irritable state

Neuropathy: Unaccepted; withdrawn; distrustful; denial of emotions; withhold and distrust love

Neurosis: Overloaded; pressured; no letting up; "can't quit"

Nodules: Frustration and resentment; need to prove self; fragile ego

Nose: Disappointment; disillusioned; despairing; powerlessness; distrustful; lack of self-belief; overly self-conscious

Nosebleeds: Overlooked; powerlessness; feeling unimportant

Numbness: Unaccepted; suppressed emotions; rejection; distrustful of intimacy; withholding and distrustful of love, withdrawn

Obesity: Food is a substitute for affection; inability to express feelings; desire for love; self-protection of the body; self-satisfying; inability to admit desires

Obsessive-compulsive: Fear something bad will happen; fear of sickness or contamination; fear of harming self/others; perfectionism; not good enough; unloved; uncared for; abandonment; unresolved past hurt from unsupportive home

Osteomyelitis: Unsupported; frustration and anger; running on empty; desire for approval

Osteoporosis: Unsupported; betrayed; fatigued; depleted; unloved; difficulty feeling love; need for control

Ovaries: Desire for love and respect; not good enough; fear rejection; inadequacy in sexual role; loneliness; unsupported; unappreciated; question female identity; anger

Overeating (compulsive): Tension; material/emotional lack; crave closeness; put on "emotional armor," a symbol of power; desire to "throw one's weight around"; emotional energy based on anger and resentment

Overweight: Insecure; self-rejection; self-protection of the body; desire for love and fulfillment; self-satisfying; suppressed emotions; unexpressed, misperceived, and inappropriate feelings

Pain: Belief that God is trying to get your attention; suppressed anger; hurtful relationship; guilt; unbalanced; frustration

Paget's disease: Uncared for; abandoned; unsupported; deprived of affection and emotion as a child

Palsy: Stagnation; inability to move forward; rigid-thinking; guilt, rejection; unforgiving; fear; uncertainty; insecure; fear as a child

Pancreas: Judged; guilt; low self-esteem; suppressed laughter; lack of self-value; betrayed; "everyone owes me"; joylessness; refuses joy; selfish; rejected; despondent about life; anger; resentful; judgmental; rejecting of others; bitterness

Panic attacks: Overwhelming fear; neglected; abandonment; fear; lack of control; desire to make things right; afraid bad things will happen; fear of death; distrustful; unresolved past trauma

Paralysis: Overwhelmed by responsibility; overly burdened; subconscious desire to escape; fear of the future; inadequacy; lack of self-control; chaotic childhood; unable to change bad situations

Paralysis (left arm): Difficulty receiving from others; unaccepted

Paralysis (right arm): Difficulty giving; ineffective in life; resistance to an unexplained stubbornness; tension of the mind

Paranoid: Afraid to trust others; fear of being hurt; unforgiving; fear that everyone will hurt you; fear of intimacy; hurt by important people in the past; unresolved past trauma

Parasites: Overwhelmed; allow others to control you; fear of independence; fear of failure; distrustful; never good enough

Parathyroid: Anger; anxiety; worry; resentment; afraid to do things

Parkinson's disease: Desire full control, fear not being in control; vulnerable; unsafe and uncared for; loneliness; lack of faith in life

Pelvis: Avoid emotional/social/sexual connection; shame; lack of confidence; unfulfilled ambitions; raised in oppressive home

Penis: Likes power/dominating others; anxious about sexual performance; ignored/devalued by family; inability to make a difference; need to prove self

Peptic ulcer: Unworthiness; people-pleaser; not good enough; suppressed anger; fear; nervousness; fear of failure

Phlebitis: Trapped; no way out; life's problems seem unsolvable

Phobias: Fear something bad will happen; unsafe; distrustful; unprotected; unloved; unsupported by important people in your life; afraid of losing control; unresolved past trauma

Pineal gland: Corresponds with inner seeing and hearing; refusal to receive new understanding and enlightenment; misuse of faith; discouraged; lack of direction; lack of intuition, motivation, imagination, enlightenment, and energy; out of balance

Pink eye: Frustration; anger at present situation; wanting to obscure unpleasant realities

Pimples: Unresolved frustration; past anger resurfacing; self-disapproval

Pituitary gland: Unhappy and disappointed in life; out of control; bad luck/misfortune follow you; negative thinking; distrustful; unworthiness

Plantar wart: Frustration with present/future; anger; lack of confidence; distrustful

Pleurisy: Antagonism and hostility

Pneumonia: Weariness; desperation; unsupported; suppressed grief/loss; distrustful; unresolved hurts from past

Poison oak or ivy: Unsupported; defenseless; powerlessness; raised in restrictive, oppressive home

Polio: Betrayed; unsupported; physically restricted; fear of scarcity; raised in unsupportive home

Polyps: Emotionally trapped in the past; refusal to release past emotion; can't move forward; unemotional; fearful; unsafe; distrustful

Postnasal drip: Crying on inside; suppressed grief; victim mentality

Premenstrual syndrome (PMS): Relinquish power to others; reject feminine aspect of self; anger and despair

Prostate cancer: Repressed anger at being restricted

Prostate problems: Conflicted about sex, unresolved anger; can't let go of the past; fear of aging; want to give up; suppressed emotions, unthinking; depleted; sexually-focused; sluggish memory; selfishness

Psoriasis: Emotional insecurity; unaccountable for feelings; past hurts; fear of being hurt; resigned to current circumstances

Pyorrhea: Anger at self for indecisiveness

Racing mind (fast thinking; see also ADD): Life out of your control; stupid; less than; inability to fit in; negative self-perception; not allowed to think for self; must prove self; not good enough

Rage (explosive fits): Anger; must prove self; others emotionally unavailable; fear of showing true feelings; unloved; abusive and strict upbringing; not good enough; distrustful; inability to get close; hurt others before being hurt by them; unresolved past trauma

Rash: Easily irritated by people/things; can't move forward in life; insecure; immature; attention-hog; guilt; shame

Respiratory problems (see also Lungs): Unloved; loneliness; sadness; unaccepted; unworthiness; unaccepted; suppressed emotions; grief; unfulfilled ambitions

Restless leg syndrome: Desire to be in control; anger; lack of control; helplessness; overwhelmed; suppressed emotions

Rheumatism: Resentment; desire for revenge; victimized; bitterness; unloving of self/others; rejected; unloved; resists change; ruminates

Right side of body issues: Masculine side; helplessness; unable to help others; unable to let go

Sacroiliac problems: In the wrong place (job, city, relationship, etc.); suppressed/conflicted sexuality; at risk; lack of direction, stuck

Sciatica: Anxiety regarding creative abilities; double-minded; sexual frustration; money concerns; ignored; defeated

Sclerosis: Repressed anger/rage; self-disapproval; guilt; shame; distrustful; at risk; burdened; helplessness/hopelessness; overloaded by responsibility; loneliness; unsupported

Seizures: Pressured; overwhelmed; fearful, despairing, anger; desire to run away; unreasonable expectations as a child

Separation anxiety: Abandonment; fear of being alone; uncared for; past trauma; unresolved past emotion, especially fears

Sex organs: Apathetic; separated

Shins: Unsafety/insecure; abandoned; uncared for as a child; indecisive; resistant to change; false beliefs and values

Shingles: Fear things won't work out; overly sensitive; tension; self-hostility

Shoulders: Burdened; stressed by responsibility; difficulty setting boundaries; surpressed emotions; unfulfilled desires; difficulty expressing emotions; issues with intimacy; loneliness

Shoulders (hunched and sloped): Life is a struggle

Shoulders (round): Hopelessness; helplessness

Sickle cell anemia: Inferiority; unloved; past hurts; self-rejecting; unworthiness

Sinus: Desire to control/make decisions for others; rejected; dominating/possessive; easily irritated _

Sinus (sinusitis): Resentful; anger at people close to you; dissastisfaction with actions of others

Skin: Insecure; embarrassed; shame; guilt; inferiority; lack of peace and harmony; unsettling emotions; annoyed; anxiety; easily irritated; unforgiveness, critical, unloved

Skin (dermatitis): Easily irritated by people/situations; suppressed irritation; anger; fearful; insecurities create suppressed emotions; raised in chronic dysfunctional family

Skin (disease): Unresolved irritation; criticized; insecure; disturbed by trivial things; impatience; bored; unsettled

Skin (skin rashes): Inner conflicts resurfacing; easily irritated by people/situations; frustrated; unproductive

Sleep apnea: Disappointment; unforgiveness; bitterness; hypersensitivity; fear of rejection; unloved; guilt; shame; resists joy; suppressed emotions

Slipped disc: Indecisiveness; unsupported

Small intestine: Lost; vulnerable; abandoned; absent-minded; insecure; distrustful; doubting; poor self-image; unappreciated; easily overwhelmed

Small pox: Rage over restrictions; resentful of rules; self-critical

Snoring: Brokenhearted; overly responsible; blamed; can't let go

Sore throat: Suppressed emotional needs; anger about loss; isolated from others

Spasms: Fearful about life; suppressed emotions

Sperm count (low): Unconscious belief of being unprepared to parent; lack of desire for children; inadequate as a parent; not good enough as male, fearful

Spinal meningitis: Unresolved rage; suppressed anger

Spleen: Lack of self-love; unloved; rejected; emotional conflicts; intense anger/antagonism; worry; low self-esteem; lack of control; overly sympathetic; uncertainty; deprived of good things; brooding

Sprains: Resistant and unable to change direction; struggle moving forward

Sterility: Tension; coldness; distant; emotional conflict; fearul; distrustful

Stomach: Insecure/unsafe; fearful of new ideas; lack of affection; unhappiness; condemn success of others; nervousness; disgusted; impatient; obsessed with material things

Strep throat: Unfairly judged/criticized; difficulty expressing self; resentful; suppress expression of needs; deprived of needs; unsupported

Stroke: Rejecting; overly resistant; unloved; uncared for; overloaded with pressures; desire to give up; self-critical

Stuttering: Dares not stand up for emotions; difficulty expressing self; perfectionism; emotionally insecure; people-pleaser; fear of authority figures

Sty: Unable to see the best in other people; unresolved anger

Suicidal: Inability to resolve problems; pessimistic about the future; discouraged; ambivalent; "everyone would be better off without me"

Swelling: Suppressed negative emotions; trapped in the past; fearful of the future

Tailbone: Unduly concerned with material needs/survival needs

Tardive dyskinesia: Failure; can't move forward; lack of confidence

Teeth: Undecisive; lack of confidence and assertiveness; overwhelming responsibilities; rescuer; resists intimacy

Teeth (toothache): Undeserving; responsibility overload; lack of confidence; shame

Tendons: Fear of letting go; self-rejecting; distrustful; desire to be in control; unable to forgive self; can't move forward

Testicles: Fear of: losing masculinity; overly responsible as a child;, powerlessness; restricted, self-doubting; lack of confidence

Thighs: Can't move forward; fearful of the future; inadequacy; unloved

Throat: Suppressed emotions; criticized often; suppressed emotional hurts; dosen't get own way; confusion; lack of discernment; lack of wisdom

Throat (lump in throat): Grief; unsafe; difficulty with self-expression

Thrush: Anger from poor choices; distrustful; disgusted; negative thinking

Thymus: Persecuted; picked on; "life is unfair"; unprotected; unworthy of good things

Thyroid: Fearful of self-expression; frustration/anxiety; lack of discernment; paranoid; muddled thinking; suppressed emotion

Tinnitus: Refuse to acknowledge inner voice; unlistening; hearing loss due to trauma; verbally abused; suppressed emotions

TMJ (see jaw problems)

Toes: Worrying over details; lack of confidence; ineffective; distrustful

Tongue: Untruthful; joyless; overly responsible; unheard; blamed; bad things spoken over you

Tonsils: Fear; anger; irritation; don't get own way; fear self-expression

Traumatic brain injury (TBI): Overly emotional; physical and cellular memory trauma

Tremors: Fearful; insecure; fearful of uncertainty; stagnant; immobilized; lack of control, self-defeating; unpredictable/devastating home life

Tuberculosis: Selfishness; possessiveness; cruel to others

Tumors (false growth): Suppressed hurts; remorse; hate; anger; false values; pride; unforgiven; resentment; distant from parents

Ulcers: Worry over details; things not going your way; anxiety; fearful; desire for vengeance; helplessness; powerlessness; overly pressured

Underweight: Worry; fearful; distrustful; extreme tension

Urinary infections: Blame others; easily irritated; lack of confidence; can't let go; hopelessness; abandonment/vulnerability issues; unloved

Uterus: Unresolved feelings toward mother; negative feelings toward creativity

Vagina: Sexual guilt; self-rejection; loss; not good enough; fear of sex/vulnerability; raised in judgmental home

Varicose veins: Tension; desire to run away; discouraged; overburdened; negative; resistant to truth; overburdened

Venereal disease: Need to be punished; guilt over sexual history

Vertigo: Difficulty changing negative behavior; overwhelming pressures; joylessness; inability to deal with difficult realities; unsafe; heavy demands

Viral infections: Bitterness; inability to recognize good things in life; multiple traumas; too many responsibilities; resentful; fear of being sick

Vomiting: Rejecting unpleasant realities; disgusted

Warts: Inability to recognize good things in life; guilt; self-disgust; unloved; not good enough

Whooping cough: Supressed emotions; unloved; unappreciated; unimportant/unworthy; ashamed of self/opinions; raised by perfectionistic parents

Yeast infections: Unresolved hurts; resentful; lack of confidence; unable to love, support, or accept self; denial of own needs

REFERENCES

References for this section are taken from Craig's years of clinical observation and with grateful permission from the following:

Truman, Karol K., *Feelings Buried Alive Never Die…* (St. Geroge, UT: Olympus Distributing, 1991), 220–264.

American Psychiatric Association, *Diagnostic Statistical Manual of Mental Disorders*, 5th Edition: DSM-5 (Washington, DC: American Psychiatric Publishing, 2016).

Clark, Randy and Miller, Craig, *Finding Victory When Healing Doesn't Happen* (Mechanicsburg, PA: Apostolic Network of Global Awakening, 2015), 143–181.

STEPS FOR HEALING PRAYERS— PUTTING THE STEPS TOGETHER

WHEN TO USE EACH PRAYER STEP

PRAYERS FOR INITIAL HEALING:

Step I: Prayer for Healing (use at any time for any healing need)

PRAYERS FOR REVEALING AND RELEASING EMOTIONS, MEMORIES, AND OTHER ISSUES:

Step II: Prayers for Releasing Soul Traumas (use when healing doesn't occur)

Step III: Releasing the Offender and False Responsibility (use after Step II)

Step IV: Determining Completion of Healing Memory (use after Step II and III, to gauge whether inner healing is completed before ending session or moving on to another memory)

Step V: Releasing Trauma Love Hug (use simultaneously with any of the other steps, especially Step II, or prayers to release suppressed emotions and memories)

PRAYERS FOR RESTORATION OF THE SPIRIT, SOUL, AND BODY:

Step V: The Love Hug (use after Step II is complete to receive greater revelation, increased mind/body integration, and a greater sense of God's love and comfort).

1. Releasing Trauma Love Hug

2. Comfort and Revelation Love Hug

3. Restoring the Mind-Body Connection Love Hug

Step VI: Additional Healing Prayers

(You may photocopy the steps to use as needed.)

FOR ANY HEALING NEED:

STEP I. PRAYER FOR HEALING

1. *Ask:* What is your name? What do you need prayer for?

2. *Ask:* What is the amount [intensity level] you feel the condition in your mind/body? (Use a pain scale of 0–10, with zero being no pain at all and ten being intense pain.)

3. *Command:* the emotions, pain, and physical condition to leave, in Jesus's name.

4. *Ask:* What is the amount [intensity level] you feel the condition now in your mind/body? (Use the same 0–10 scale.)

5. *Praise* God for any healing. Repeat steps 1–5 for more healing.

6. *Instruct:* Teach the person how to believe for healing by focusing on God's Word, not on their pain or condition. Encourage them to give Jesus all their hurt.

If Healing Doesn't Occur: continue to Step II

© Craig Miller 2018 (www.insightsfromtheheart.com)

STEP II: PRAYERS FOR RELEASING TRAUMA

1. Ask: "When did you first remember experiencing this condition or feeling?"

1a. If the memory/reason for condition is **known**...

Ask: "Describe what happened and how it made you feel?" Proceed to #2

1b. If the memory/reason for the condition is **unknown**...

Ask/Pray: "Describe your feelings of living with the condition." Pray to recall early memories that produced similar feelings. Proceed to #2

2. Ask: "Thinking of the past memory, rate the amount of hurt you feel the mind/body condition." (0–10 scale)

3. Instruct: "Picture Jesus [or another safe person] in the memory standing between you and the offending person/situation protecting/hugging you [see Step V Love Hug below] or hugging you within a protective bubble."

4. Pray: "In Jesus's name, curse the emotional, physical, sight, hearing, and cellular memory trauma."

5. Pray: Declare healing to the heart/mind/body, in Jesus's name.

6. Ask: "Rate the amount of hurt in your mind/body now." (0–10 pain scale)

7. Praise God for any healing or expected healing.

8. If healing does not happen: *expand your search* for earlier trauma issues and repeat 1–8, with the option to use Step V (Love Hug and love pat).

If healing happens: option to continue with Step III and Step IV.

9. Instruct: Teach the person how to believe for healing by focusing on God's Word, not on their condition. Encourage them to give Jesus all of their hurt.

STEP III. RELEASING THE OFFENDER AND FALSE RESPONSIBILITY

1. Instruct: The prayer minister will say to the afflicted person, "Picture Jesus [or any safe person] standing between you and the offender/situation. With Jesus [or any safe person] protecting you, say these words out loud, as if you were talking to the offender."

- I didn't like what you did to me.

- What you did to me was unfair.

- You made me feel (hurt, sad, angry, helpless, etc.)

- I realize that I now have choices.

- I choose to give Jesus my feelings of hurt and pain.

- It is not my responsibility to carry these feelings anymore.

- I choose to not allow these feelings to have any more authority over me.

- I choose to give what you did to me to Jesus; you have no more authority over my feelings.

- I choose to forgive you, so you have no more control over my life.

- I repent for taking on any false responsibility for this situation.

- I choose to let go of trying to fix you or this situation.

- I realize you did not know how to love me, which is not my fault.

- Heavenly Father, I choose to get love from You now.

- Heavenly Father, fill my heart with Your love in a way my (parents) couldn't.

- Thank You, Jesus, for my freedom and my healing.

© Craig Miller 2018 (www.insightsfromtheheart.com)

STEP IV: DETERMINE COMPLETION OF MEMORY HEALING

This step is helpful to determine if the unhealthy emotion is fully released, or if a past traumatic memory is complete healed, before stopping the ministry or moving on to deal with another memory.

1. After the healing of each past memory, have the person picture a younger image of themselves in that memory.

2. The prayer minister should ask, "Now that you feel that memory is healed, when you think of the earlier image of you in that memory, what do you see on your face? A smile, a frown, or a flat look?"

2a. **If it is a smile:** Ask the person, "When you think of yourself in that past memory, do you believe this statement is true or false: 'The situation is over and I can feel safe now in that memory'?"

If they say the statement is true, have them thank Jesus for their healing. This session can end or continue to another memory.

If they say the statement is false, continue to #3 below.

2b. **If it is a frown or a flat look:** Ask them what they are still feeling in that memory. **Continue to #3 below.**

3. Repeat 1 through 7 of **Step II: Prayers for Releasing Trauma** simultaneously with Step V: Releasing Trauma Love Hug.

4. After you pray and the trauma is considered healed or diminished, repeat steps 1–3 above until the person imagines themselves with a smile and feels safe in that past memory.

If the person still cannot imagine a smile after several prayers, *expand your search* to a previous memory with similar feelings, then repeat steps 1–3 of this section.

STEP V: THE LOVE HUG—THREE METHODS FOR SOUL/SPIRIT RELEASE AND RESTORATION

1. Releasing Trauma Love Hug

Instructions: Use the Love Hug (and love pat) when people feel stuck, numb, blank, confused, unable to identify emotions/memories/thoughts, unable to feel love from others or from God, or have general negative thoughts and feelings.

The prayer minister can demonstrate the technique for the afflicted person while saying,

1. "You can do the Love Hug by crossing your arms over your chest, resting your hands on your arm or bicep, as you think of Jesus [or another safe person] giving you a hug."

2. "Continue with the love pat by gently patting one hand then the other on your arm or bicep as you think of Jesus [or another safe person] giving you a 'love pat,' letting you know how much you are loved. You will alternate each hand patting your arm, i.e., right, left, right, left. Gently pat at double the speed of your relaxed heart rate." (Or the prayer minister can place a hand on each shoulder and gently give a love pat.)

Option to say: "This love pat naturally promotes the same biological functions created by God to help your mind sort through and release unwanted or blocked emotion and memory. It will encourage a sense of release, calm, and healing in your mind and body."

© Craig Miller 2018 (www.insightsfromtheheart.com)

2. Comfort and Revelation Love Hug

Instructions: Use this Love Hug (and love pat) after releasing trauma to promote peace, calm, confidence, a sense of love, revelation, guidance, direction, and reassurance from God.

The prayer minister can demonstrate the technique for the afflicted person while saying:

1. "You can do the Love Hug by crossing your arms over your chest, resting your hands on your arm or bicep, as you think of Jesus [or another safe person] giving you a hug."

2. "Continue with the love pat by gently patting one hand then the other on your arm or bicep as you think of Jesus [or another safe person] giving a 'love pat,' letting you know how much you are loved. You will alternate each hand patting your arm, i.e., right, left, right, left. Gently pat at double the speed of your relaxed heart rate." (Or the prayer minister can place a hand on each shoulder and gently give a love pat.)

Option to say: "This love pat naturally promotes the same biological functions created by God to help your mind receive a sense of peace, confidence, love, revelation, direction, and reassurance."

3. Restoring the Mind-Body Connection Love Hug

Instructions: Use this Love Hug (and love pat) to promote mind-body integration and the healing of conditions associated with mental/emotional shutdown and mind/body/spirit disconnect.

The prayer minister can demonstrate the technique for the afflicted person while saying:

1. "You can do the Love Hug by crossing your arms over your chest, resting your hands on your arm or bicep, as you think of Jesus [or another safe person] giving you a hug."

2. "Continue with the love pat by gently patting one hand then the other on your arm or bicep as you think of Jesus [or another safe person] giving a 'love pat,' letting you know how much you are loved. You will alternate each hand patting your arm, i.e., right, left, right, left. Gently pat at the speed of your relaxed heart rate." (Or the prayer minister can place a hand on each shoulder and gently give a love pat.)

Option to say: "This love pat naturally promotes the same biological functions created by God to help the potential integration of both sides of the brain for mind-body connection, integration, and healing."

RESTORING THE MIND-BODY CONNECTION PRAYERS

This is a suggested prayer that can be modified to accommodate the condition or circumstance. Have the afflicted person repeat this prayer:

In the name of Jesus, I curse the condition of _____ that has harmed my mind. I forgive myself for my part in the injury, and I forgive any other persons responsible for my injury. I repent for receiving and accepting any part of this condition or diagnosis. I curse any emotional, physical, or cellular memory trauma, as well as all symptoms and complications associated with this injury.

Prayer minister to pray:

In the name of Jesus, I curse the disconnect between [afflicted person's name] mind and body, and any emotional, mental, medical, or physical dysfunction that is causing this disunion. In the name of Jesus, I command the electrical, chemical, magnetic, hormonal, and neurological frequencies in every cell in the mind and body to become in harmony and in balance. In Jesus's name, I command the mind and body of [afflicted person's name] to become healed, become integrated, and be united to function as God intended. In Jesus's name, I declare [afflicted person's name] to receive God's spirit of life, light, love, and peace. I pray for the blood of Jesus to bring healing and wholeness to their mind and body. Thank you, Jesus, for healing.

VI. ADDITIONAL PRAYERS

ADD/ADHD, BIPOLAR, DYSLEXIA, AND OTHER CONDITIONS ORIGINATING BEFORE BIRTH

Instructions:

Ask the afflicted person to close their eyes and, on a scale of 0–10, rate how much their mind feels as if it is sad, frantic, racing, overwhelmed, or unbalanced. (Zero being complete health, 10 being extreme affliction.)

Ask the person to place their hands on their stomach.

Ask them to picture themselves in the womb, with Jesus placing His hands on them. The prayer minister can place a hand on the prayee's head and lower back. (Always ask permission before initiating contact.)

Ask the afflicted person to repeat after you:

In the name of Jesus, I curse the condition of [_____] that has passed down to me through my mother's womb from the previous generations. I forgive my mother, father, and the generations before them for passing on the condition of [_____]. I renounce this condition and do not give it permission or authority to be a part of my life anymore. I repent for receiving and accepting any part of this condition or the diagnosis given to me. In Jesus's name, I curse any symptoms or complications associated with this diagnosis. I accept Jesus in my heart and I receive Your Spirit of life, love, peace, wholeness, and restoration of my mind and body. Thank You, Jesus, for my healing.

This simpler prayer may be repeated by a child, or at any time by an adult:

I forgive you, Mother and Father, for any condition you transferred to me that is not of God. I do not accept this condition in my mind or body. Thank You, God, for restoring my health, as it is in heaven.

Next, the prayer minister can pray this prayer over the afflicted person:

In Jesus's name, I renounce the condition of [_____] and give it no more authority. In Jesus's name, I curse any utero trauma and command the electrical, chemical, magnetic, hormonal, and neurological frequencies in every cell of the mind and body to come into alignment and balance, with proper integration and polarity, as it is in heaven. In Jesus's name, I declare peace and healthy functioning over the mind and body. Thank You, Jesus, for Your healing.

Ask the afflicted person to close their eyes and, on a scale of 0–10, rate how much their mind feels as if it is sad, frantic, racing, overwhelmed, or unbalanced. (Zero being complete health, 10 being extreme affliction.) As the number decreases, repeat numbers 1–6 above until the mind feels at zero, or as close as possible.

If the number does not decrease or the mind has minimal improvement, continue by releasing past trauma symptons with the following:

Ask the afflicted person for more information about any trauma, hurt, worry, or extreme burdens they had or currently are experiencing. Pray using Step II of the Steps for Healing Prayer.

After the healing prayer, ask the afflicted person to close their eyes and rate, on a scale of 0–10 (10 is the worst), how much their mind feels as if it is sad, frantic, racing, overwhelmed, or unbalanced. As the number decreases, repeat the aforementioned numbers 1–6 until they rate their mind at zero, or as close as possible.

CANCER OR OTHER DISEASES (THE AFFLICTED PERSON CAN READ OR REPEAT AFTER THE PRAYER MINISTER):

In the name of Jesus, I curse the diagnosis spoken over me and cast out the seed, spirit, and root of [condition's name]. I curse any generational spirits or roots that have carried this condition. I repent for accepting this diagnosis and forgive the healthcare professionals for giving the diagnosis.

I forgive my parents and the generations before them for any involvement with this condition. In Jesus's name, I curse the spirit of death, fear, rejection, abandonment, and any other emotional and physical trauma from the past and present that has contributed to the condition.

In Jesus's name, I command all organs, bones, and tissues affected by this condition to be restored to healthy functioning and command the electrical, chemical, magnetic, hormonal, and neurological frequencies in every cell in my mind and body to become in harmony and balance. In Jesus's name, I curse the unhealthy prion cells in the body and declare healthy cells to be restored to normal functioning in all affected areas. In Jesus's name, I declare over my body and mind the Spirit of life, love, acceptance, peace, the light of God, and the full restoration of my mind and body to function normally as I live in the belief that I am healed. Thank You, Jesus, for my healing.

© Craig Miller 2018 (www.insightsfromtheheart.com)

HEAVENLY FATHER'S BLESSING

The prayer minister can place a hand on the afflicted person's head and say this blessing prayer. This prayer can be modified to accommodate any condition or circumstance.

Your heavenly Father wants to say to you, "I see you and I am very proud of you. I think very highly of you, I will always believe in you, and I will always love you, no matter what you have done—because that is how I really feel about you. I do not condemn you. I want to grant My favor over your life and give back to you what you have lost. I declare great blessings over you and I look forward to seeing you grow and succeed in life. I want you to trust Me and to look to Me for the guidance and love I would like to give you. I love you. I am your heavenly Daddy."

SPIRITUAL WARFARE PRAYER

The prayer minister can pray this prayer if anyone sees, feels, or senses a sudden darkness, unusual fear, shadows, the movement of objects, or oddly intense behaviors with the afflicted person.

In the authority I have in Jesus, I command this spirit of [_____] to be bound and sent away. I plead the blood of Jesus over [afflicted person's name] and, in the name of Jesus, I declare peace into their mind and body. Thank You, Jesus, for Your protection.

© Craig Miller 2018 (www.insightsfromtheheart.com)

PRAYERS TO RELEASE GENERATIONAL CONDITIONS AND CURSES

This includes medical conditions, mental illness, suicide attempts, the occult, and other demonic acitivity. The prayer minister can pray or the afflicted person can repeat prayer.

In the name of Jesus, I declare the blood of Jesus to come between me and the generations before me as a wall of separation. I cancel every assignment of darkness and remove every right of [name the condition] to afflict me. I renounce and give no more authority for this generational issue or cause to be in my life. I forgive the generations before me and receive the blood of Jesus to cleanse my mind and body and call to me my righteous inheritance and blessings of that generation. Thank You, Jesus, for my freedom.

© Craig Miller 2018 (www.insightsfromtheheart.com)

ABOUT THE AUTHOR

CRAIG MILLER has been ministering and counseling in church, medical, and mental health settings since 1980. He is a licensed Christian therapist and co-founder of Masterpeace Counseling in Tecumseh, Michigan. He holds a master's degree in social work from Michigan State University and a master's degree in health services administration from the University of Detroit. He has served as a lay minister and as the director of social work for Herrick Hospital in Tecumseh.

Experiencing his own miraculous physical healing deepened Craig's passion to help people receive healing and restoration through teaching, imparting, and ministering the love and healing power of Jesus. Craig ministers to the spirit and soul (mind, will, and emotions) for God to identify the root causes that block healing of physical or emotional conditions. He also teaches and ministers through TV and radio appearances, speaking at national healing conferences, healing services, and through his other books: *When Feelings Don't Come Easy*, *When Your Mate Is Emotionally Unavailable*, *Declaring Your Worth*, and *Finding Victory When Healing Doesn't Happen*, which he coauthored with Randy Clark.

For more information about Craig, go to
www.insightsfromtheheart.com.